Psychotherapy and the Treatment of Cancer Patients

Psychotherapy and the Treatment of Cancer Patients addresses the need for a more integrated care of cancer patients within hospitals, which pays attention to the mental anguish as well as physical distress caused by the disease. This book is based on Lawrence Goldie's own research with cancer patients, which has shown that psychoanalytic psychotherapy together with general medical care can significantly help dying patients cope with the pain and suffering associated with the disease.

Drawing on this research, the book advocates a more holistic approach to the cancer patient and suggests ways in which more expert attention might be provided through awareness, training and resources. The book describes the innovative approach of applying the psychoanalytic psychotherapeutic approach within the hospital context to help individuals cope with cancer. As well as an overview of cancer and the therapeutic approach, topics covered include:

- The impact of cancer on hospital relationships
- Cancer in different areas of the body and mind
- 'Mind-bending pain'
- Dread and trauma – on being told the truth
- Psychoanalytic psychotherapy in the NHS 'general' hospital
- Examining group processes in hospital

Psychotherapy and the Treatment of Cancer Patients challenges the existing orthodoxies about palliative care and points to ways in which the principles and methods of psychoanalysis can be applied successfully to cancer care within the hospital context.

Lawrence Goldie is a consultant psychiatrist and psychoanalytic psychotherapist. He has published widely on a variety of topics including hypnosis, epilepsy, sleep patterns in infants, intracranial bruits and on the subject of 'attention and inattention'. His psychiatric training was at the Institute of Psychiatry in London and while at the Institute of Psychoanalysis he was supervised by Dr Wilfred Bion, who inspired his work.

Jane Desmarais teaches in the department of English & Comparative Literature at Goldsmiths College, University of London. She has published in the fields of literature, the visual arts, and psychoanalysis.

Psychotherapy and the Treatment of Cancer Patients

Bearing cancer in mind

Lawrence Goldie
with Jane Desmarais

Routledge
Taylor & Francis Group

LONDON AND NEW YORK

First published 2005
by Routledge
27 Church Road, Hove, East Sussex BN3 2FA

Simultaneously published in the USA and Canada
by Routledge
270 Madison Avenue, New York, NY 10016

Routledge is an imprint of the Taylor & Francis Group

Typeset in Times by Keystroke, Jacaranda Lodge, Wolverhampton
Printed and bound in Great Britain by MPG Books Ltd, Bodmin
Paperback cover design by Lisa Dynan

This publication has been produced with paper manufactured to
strict environmental standards and with pulp derived from
sustainable forests.

British Library Cataloguing in Publication Data
A catalogue record for this book is available from the British Library

Library of Congress Cataloging in Publication Data
Goldie, Lawrence, 1923–
    Psychotherapy and the treatment of cancer patients : bearing
cancer in mind / Lawrence Goldie with Jane Desmarais.
        p. ; cm.
    Includes bibliographical references and index.
    ISBN 1-58391-857-4 (pbk) – ISBN 1-58391-856-6 (hbk)
    1. Cancer–Psychological aspects. 2. Cancer–Palliative
treatment. 3. Psychoanalytic psychotherapy. 4. Terminal
care. 5. Cancer–Patients–Hospital care.
    [DNLM: 1. Neoplasms–therapy. 2. Hospitals. 3. Palliative
Care–organization & administration. 4. Psychoanalytic
Therapy.] I. Desmarais, Jane Haville. II. Title.
    RC271.P79G65 2005
    616.99'406—dc22
                                                    2005001709

ISBN 1-58391-857-4 (pbk)
ISBN 1-58391-856-6 (hbk)

The art of living well and dying well are one.
(Epicurus)

Contents

Preface

There were many threads that drew me to the work that I did at the Royal Marsden Hospital in 1972. At the time I lived near the Sutton branch of the hospital and a relative of my wife was admitted to this hospital. I knew Mr W quite well and I rather admired him. He was originally born in Czechoslovakia but subsequently escaped and volunteered for the British Army. He was admitted to the Royal Marsden Hospital at Sutton because he had developed cancer of the lung.

When I visited him, the Sister on the ward asked me what I did and I told her I was a psychiatrist and this led her to tell me about the pain and emotional difficulties that she had witnessed in patients. To her distress, their emotional pain was not considered. I became interested in the problems that she told me about and this resulted in my introduction to an eminent radiologist, Dr S. He asked me to join him when he was on the ward discussing patients. He was impressive when demonstrating his frankness with his patients. On one occasion he brought in a 50-year-old man. He had this patient's X-rays on the viewing box and he pointed out to the patient the cancer in his lungs. At that time patients came to the hospital at Sutton for radiological investigations and also for radiotherapy, but, as Dr S told me, the radiotherapists and radiologists did not take charge of the patients. They merely conducted investigations. The doctor in charge of the patient was the doctor who originally saw and referred the patient. As a radiologist, Dr S admitted that he was no more in a position to carry on seeing a patient than a pathologist would be, examining biopsy specimens or the blood of a patient.

Still, I was struck at this first meeting with Dr S, with how he discussed openly the cancer with the patient. There was no emotion but there was no coldness either. I recalled later that he had said that the lesion was very slow growing, and although I cannot quote his exact words it was something like 'There is nothing more that can be done'. When the patient left the room I asked Dr S 'What is the outlook for this patient?' He replied 'Well, it is very slow growing, and it will probably be something like two years or more before this patient has any symptoms or difficulties.' This was very reasonable, but what made me review his words to the patient was the discovery later that the patient had died of a heart attack the following weekend. I thought that this was because when the radiologist said there was nothing more to be done, the patient had taken this to mean that he was a hopeless case. In films and books, this is what is usually said when there is no hope for a patient, when they are about to die.

On reflection, I thought that the discussion with the patient was very limited. No one knew what the patient thought about what was being shown or said to him. I was struck by the fact that the cancer was no immediate threat to his life, and was unlikely to be so for a considerable length of time. But he died of a heart attack.

After diagnosis by the radiologist, my wife's relative, Mr W, was referred to his original doctor, and he was then transferred from the Marsden. The X-rays had shown that the cancer was in his lung and that there was no treatment for it at present. He then reverted to the care of the surgeon he had originally consulted. This surgeon did not know where to place him so he put him in a general ward in another hospital.

I discovered where Mr W had been transferred and went to visit him. The ward seemed to contain a mixture of senile patients and mental patients. I spoke to him and he was, as usual, polite and seemingly quite accepting of the diagnosis, without complaining about being in that particular ward. As I was leaving, I was approached by the young House Surgeon who asked to speak to me, because she said Mr W had been asking her to provide him with enough tablets for him to be able to take his own life. She was quite confused and did not know what to say to Mr W or what to do about his request. I was shocked and realised this other side of him. He was in despair, feeling himself abandoned and relegated to this ward, where no treatment was taking place. From his point of view, the ward was full of people who were hopeless and mentally disturbed.

When I first started working at the Marsden, there was always the issue of who was ultimately responsible for the patient, especially when there were several different teams involved. Often the responsibility for the patient was disavowed, and it fell upon the doctor who had originally referred the patient. The doctor or surgeon, as in the case of Mr W, often no longer had an interest, or any means of treating the patient. It was quite ridiculous really, as with Mr W, to refer the patient back to a doctor who had no further interest or treatment resources. He did eventually return home, but he was very depressed and miserable, and he developed a heart condition, dying of a coronary thrombosis. He seemed to me to be very miserable, depressed and unhappy. I never forgot what I thought was really quite tragic: that such a brave man, who fought in another country's army, should feel so hopeless, abandoned and useless that he would want to commit suicide.

I was asked by Dr S to come on to the wards to look round the hospital, and to make any observations that I cared to about what was happening. I spoke to the sisters on the wards. At that time, I had a friend, Mr C, who was a surgeon at the hospital. He specialised in surgery of the abdomen and large bowel. He told me how he was spending a lot of his time with his outpatients discussing their emotional and sexual difficulties. He said that these discussions were becoming increasingly commonplace, that he was discussing the issues of sex and sexuality more than their surgical condition. Patients feared that they had cancer of the bowel because they felt something intruding in their rectum. Mr C would see them in the clinic and perform a rectal examination, only to discover in the majority of cases, that these men had enlarged prostates. He would then have discussions with these patients about their 'sex life' and discover that they had ceased to have sexual intercourse. He thought that this was the main reason for the prostatic enlargement. As a consequence, he approached me to take over from him the discussion of the sexual problems of patients who came to his clinic.

After a while, along with another radiotherapist, Mr C recommended to the Marsden Hospital Committee that a survey was required of the psychiatric needs of the hospital. Knowing me quite well, they both suggested that I should conduct a survey of their psychiatric needs. It was agreed, and money was set aside for one year when I would do the survey and submit a report at the end of that time. The House Governor asked me if, whilst I was doing this survey, I would also undertake to see any cases that might be referred, which I agreed to. I had no intention at that time of having a permanent appointment with the hospital and it was with considerable difficulty that I managed to fit in time to see patients, as I was already fully occupied with treating patients elsewhere.

After it was agreed that I should do this survey, I received letters from individual members of the Committee expressing considerable fears and doubts about the plan. One letter asked me not to go round the hospital telling patients that they were going to die! I was also told by some of the Committee that there had been very strong opposition to the idea of a psychiatrist in the hospital, let alone one inclined towards psychoanalytic psychotherapy. Some thought that it was completely unnecessary to have a psychiatrist, as the patients never required one. In any event they thought that their handling of patients was quite adequate. Another physician said that he had worked for a time in a psychiatric hospital, so he knew quite a lot about psychiatry. He, along with another physician who was violently opposed to psychiatry, joined a chorus of prejudice against psychiatry and psychiatrists. These two physicians, the latter one in particular, remained very cool towards me when I subsequently became a member of staff and a member of the Committee. Both of them had occasion to refer patients to me only when they had got into difficulties with them, and when they had no alternative but to ask for my help. This made me a witness to their failings, which they disliked.

I knew, therefore, when I started the survey that there were all kinds of opposition from those at the top. It was as if many feared the intrusion of a psychiatrist who would be looking at their behaviour, perhaps seeing problems that were not being attended to. They also felt, it seemed to me, that their 'patch' and their authority were being undermined by a psychiatrist. They seemed to feel that their relationship to patients was adequate. They felt confident and god-like with regard to them, and feared that this position was going to be threatened by my presence.

One radiotherapist said to the Chairman of the Committee that he did not think there was ever any necessity to have a psychiatrist see his patients. To his amazement, the Chairman told him that there were more complaints from his patients about his callous and cruel handling of them than the rest of the hospital put together. To his credit, this very eminent radiotherapist was astonished and chastened. Subsequently he referred patients to me, including his best friend. He obviously had no idea how he came over to his patients.

After three months of going round the hospital, I was asked to give a short talk and have some discussion with senior nursing staff and social workers about what I had observed. There was great general hostility towards me, and up to that point I think that I would not have been able to carry on without the support of the Matron at that time. She was a very passionate and caring person who was fully aware of the pain and suffering of the patients. A heated exchange ensued after I had given my talk. Some of the religious social workers objected and said that the patients did not require a psychiatrist. All they needed was spiritual support and religion; and if the patients had this religious conviction they would not be so afraid. The Matron, to their dismay, totally disagreed with them and said that they had two nuns in the hospital as patients, they were seriously ill, and were the most frightened of all the patients in the hospital. Nevertheless there remained some others who were deeply suspicious and opposed to my intervention. One was a Senior Sister on one of the wards, who was very religious and believed, like the social workers, that this was all the patients required. Another Senior Sister was less dogmatic, asking me what I could do that drugs could not do. She thought that all the patients needed was heavy medication, and she said quite sincerely and reasonably that she could not see what else could be done in these circumstances.

As I became more and more involved in the work of the hospital I noticed a strange atmosphere. It specialised in cancer and therefore it provided the enthusiastic doctors with the opportunity for practising medicine, for exercising both their diagnostic talents and their knowledge of remedies and surgery. It was a good place to be because there were always many interesting surgical problems, and more than enough work for the surgical staff to do. It was, in other words, a hive of activity, but with what I later realised were defences against pain. There were many meetings and statistical trials. There were morning, mid-day and evening conferences. These often were, I think, defences against the misery and the lack of success in so much of the treatment.

I realised that this hospital had an atmosphere that I had never experienced before in all the other hospitals that I had worked in. In most general hospitals there is bustle and much cheerfulness: people in plaster and on crutches, people getting over operations. Generally speaking, there is evidence of the fulfilment and gratitude of patients, and the pleasure of the staff as they are thanked and see people getting better and leaving after surgery. The occasional diagnosis of cancer and death from the disease is submerged in all the emergencies and excitement associated with them. However, in this hospital, the atmosphere was different. The activities of the doctors were displayed on notice boards announcing innumerable daily team meetings and meetings on special cancer topics. For the lay person this presented a chilling menu; for those who wanted to practise medicine and surgery an exciting programme. By contrast, there were the wards, and the patients in the corridors and in outpatients, who were sad and browbeaten, many obviously emaciated by the treatment. The appearance of many was altered in that they had lost hair. One could guess from looking at the various patients what stage of treatment, or what type of treatment, they were having. The patients almost uniformly throughout the hospital had become an underclass. The nursing attention, it must be said, was generally very good and given with great compassion and pity, but the patients were submerged in the busy hospital efficiency.

I used to think at the outset that one could not conduct psychoanalytic psychotherapy with people who are dying. One could not call them back from the dead to see if the sessions or ministrations had helped and at the beginning I did not know in what way I could be of assistance. Without exception, the patients I saw knew little about psychiatry and psychology, and still less about psychoanalysis. By applying the method and principles of psychoanalytic psychotherapy within a hospital setting I was taking an enormous chance.

In the hospital at this time, there were no psychotic patients and I did not think that any of them were neurotic. While I used to say to them I did not know in what way I could help, I did not realise that by giving them my attention and really looking at each one as an individual, hearing what they had to say, I was able to help. I was simply trying to find a way to approach those patients about their feelings about having cancer. The technique I used was uncomplicated. My aims were modest. They were encouraged to think about themselves in the company of another person, someone who was interested in what they thought and felt. I was someone who was interested in their lives, their family, their loves, their hates and their pain, their recriminations, their doubts about what would happen to the children when they were dead. Apart from my interventions, no one else looked at them and thought about them in this way in the hospital context.

The referrals came thick and fast, but initially they were mostly from the Chaplain and from the ward sisters. Many patients spoke directly to the Chaplain asking for some kind of help, no matter what their religion, and he in turn would ask me to see them. It was noteworthy that very few referrals came from the senior medical staff. Presumably the Chaplain could be spoken to about non-medical matters, whereas patients thought doctors could not be spoken to about matters other than medical. The sisters on the ward would get the junior doctors to refer patients, although many of the juniors referred patients very reluctantly, often carelessly and casually. They were never interested enough in the outcome of my meetings with the patients to enquire how they were getting on.

The sisters on most of the wards, on the other hand, became enthusiastic supporters of my work, simply because they thought that they saw changes in their patients. This grew over the year, with a very good relationship being established between myself and the nursing staff and sisters. However, when I attempted to hold seminars for the nurses, and when there was the possibility of training some of the nurses for psychotherapeutic work, there was very strong opposition from some of the sisters. It was impossible to get the nursing staff together for any regular sequence of seminars. This was also the experience of visiting psychologists and others from the Tavistock Clinic, who tried to do the same. It was paradoxical that whilst I led seminars for nurses on cancer and psychotherapy who came from hospitals all over London, the nurses in the Marsden, where the seminars were held, never came more than once or twice and never attended for a whole series.

Much has changed since I started my survey in 1972. Training has improved. A generation of 'nurse counsellors' has emerged. Some are called 'mastectomy nurses' and some are 'stoma nurses'. The first appointments at the Marsden were of nurses without any extra training, who had got into difficulties in caring for some patients. Some of these came to me asking for help but some gave up their work, feeling unable to cope with the load of emotional problems that comes for caring for those with cancer. Extra training is crucial if specialist nursing is to be successful.

I realised that there was no place for traditional psychiatry with cancer patients. The patients were normal people, who, because of the cancer, were understandably depressed and concerned. The drugs used in psychiatry seemed to me to be absolutely and completely inappropriate. As time went on I realised that all these patients were, in a sense, neglected. The defence against their pain and tribulations was becoming confused with their physical condition, and they were being treated physically rather than psychologically. What patients needed was an opportunity to talk to someone who was able to appreciate and even understand and work with some of their emotional problems.

I began my work with cancer patients, therefore, with a tremendous amount of opposition. It was a fantasy of most of my colleagues, physicians and surgeons that a patient might occasionally need to be admitted to a psychiatric hospital, but only because they were suicidally depressed. In fact this never occurred whilst I was attending the hospital. There were other doctors who were absolutely against psychiatric help because they felt that this was a slur on their positions as physicians. One made that quite explicit and felt that as a competent doctor he should be able to cope with all the mental problems as well as the physical problems and therefore was in no need of the assistance of a psychiatrist. One particular physician was obsessed and terrified when he learned that a psychiatrist might be seeing some of his patients. He thought initially that he was going to be exposed for *not* having told the patients that they were going to die.

I duly submitted my report after a year and, as a consequence, it was suggested that the hospital take on an appropriate consultant psychiatrist for a limited number of sessions with patients. The position was not advertised nor offered for occupation by me or anyone else. My report had strongly indicated the need for some form of psychological support for patients and at the same time showed that psychiatry without psychoanalytical psychotherapeutic content would be useless. But, in spite of this, the hospital continued to treat only the physical symptoms of cancer. I then worked for a further year without pay or a formal appointment. The House Governor found this situation an embarrassment, however, and he urged upon the Committee the need for someone to take up the position. In effect, this was so that I could be paid and have a formal appointment as a consultant. I was taken on, but for only half the time recommended in my report, the excuse being that there were insufficient funds. I was never given any junior staff. I was not provided with a secretary or an office. The House Governor again helped by providing me with a dictating machine and secretarial help, but only after three years was it arranged that I share a secretary and an office with the consultant urologists.

I became completely embroiled in seeing outpatients and inpatients. Some of the outpatients could be booked ahead of time for appointments, but for most of the time, I arrived at the hospital to discover whom I had to see. The demands were irresistible as all these people were very ill and I often felt I could not leave the hospital without seeing some of the referrals. Time was of the essence; two days later and the patient might no longer be alive. In my report I had recommended strongly that the hospital employ a team of psychotherapists who were experienced in dealing with the emotional problems of people, normal people hit by demanding and testing, traumatic events, but this was only ammunition to the hospital management. They opposed my recommendations for the most part, claiming that they were not 'statistical', not in line with all the other research conducted in the hospital, that is, research on the latest drugs, or on the percentage of people who got better or worse. Had I managed to tout successfully for research funds, and conducted research that produced figures and quantitative results, I would certainly have established probably a department and a base.

When I began working at the Royal Marsden in the early 1970s, I felt that I had wandered into a battlefield, with the wounded and dead lying all over the place, and with inadequate numbers to attend to the casualties. Some got help, but only a minority. Others were left to die. Sometimes it felt as if the wounded were unimportant. It was this experience which affected me so much, and I began to see the possibilities that might be afforded by giving psychoanalytic psychotherapy to people who were sick and dying. Of course, much has changed since those early days both in that hospital, and elsewhere. But it is because so much more remains to be done, in places where the dying we care for, in wards where cancer is treated, and in work with patients and relatives, that I have decided to relate my experience.

I am grateful to the many surgical and medical colleagues who gave me support and encouragement during my work at the Royal Marsden. Many constantly referred their patients to me, and were impressive in their concern for their patients, despite the disappointing results of treatment. I came to respect greatly the colleagues who were initially derisory but who were able to change their views and become instead co-operative and generous to my project. I learned most, however, from the many patients that I saw and listened to over the decades. I was continually impressed and humbled by their eloquence and reflection. They were ordinary people in extra-ordinary conditions. This book is for them.

Lawrence Goldie
London, 2004

Acknowledgements

The author wishes to thank Richard Lucas for his extremely helpful comments on draft chapters, and also Ann Bond who has kindly contributed one of her cases discussed in supervision. This book would never have been written without the support and encouragement of my wife, Silvia – to her I would like to say a special thank you.

Some of the material included in this book has been published elsewhere and the authors would like to thank the BMJ Publishing Group, the British Psychosocial Oncology Group, *Edition Selva Verlag*, and *Psychoanalytic Psychotherapy*:

Chapter 5 includes material from, L. Goldie (1989), 'Psychological Aspects of Pain Perception and the Memory of Pain' and 'Too Much Pain – The Emotional Problems Associated with Serious Illness and Its Treatment', *Pain – Research and Treatment*, 1–5, and 128–132, with permission of Edition Selva Verlag.

Chapter 6 is based on L. Goldie (1982), 'The Ethics of Telling the Patient', *Journal of Medical Ethics*, 8: 128–133, with permission of the BMJ Publishing Group.

Chapter 7 includes material from L. Goldie (1985), 'The Interdisciplinary Treatment of Cancer: Co-operation or Competition?', *Psychosocial Oncology: Proceedings of the British Psychosocial Oncology Group*, 77–85, with permission from the British Psychosocial Oncology Group and L. Goldie (1984), 'Psychoanalysis in the National Health Service General Hospital', *Psychoanalytic Psychotherapy*, 1, 2: 23–34, with permission of *Psychoanalytic Psychotherapy*.

Introduction

The idea for this book originates from my research with cancer patients, which has shown that psychoanalytic psychotherapy, together with general medical care, can significantly help dying patients cope with the pain and suffering associated with cancer. Traditionally, the dying patient is isolated, marginalised even, within the hospital environment. As if the shock and devastation of cancer are not enough, the dying patient is removed from a 'healthy' world and is administered psychotropic drugs and sedatives that are intended to suppress pain and alleviate discomfort. These drugs are not always appropriate because the patient is not suffering from an abnormal mental state but is experiencing shock and devastation, which are normal responses. My research has shown that by listening and talking to cancer patients, creative, psychotherapeutic exchanges produce a new sense of integration for the patient, and may permit the resolution of longstanding conflicts. In some cases, patients are able to achieve a philosophical acceptance of their own life and its termination by cancer.

Psychotherapy and the Treatment of Cancer Patients: Bearing Cancer in Mind is the first study in psycho-oncology to embrace psychoanalytical concepts as part of the treatment of cancer patients who are not psychiatric cases. Drawing on research conducted over nearly two decades, it proposes a radical re-evaluation of both cancer care and the application of psychoanalytic–psychotherapeutic ideas in this context. The preoccupation with the unconscious processes of individuals who are dying is a distinctive feature of this work and a principal aim has been to offer new insights in plain language (stripped of medical and psychoanalytic jargon) into the relationship between mental and physiological events.

I interrupted my studies for a BSc Honours degree in psychology to join the Royal Air Force and become a pilot. On demobilisation I qualified in medicine and subsequently became a consultant psychiatrist and psychoanalytic psychotherapist in the National Health Service at the postgraduate Institutes of London University. My psychiatric training was at the Institute of Psychiatry at the Maudsley Hospital, where I conducted neurophysiological research in the department of Sir Denis Hill. This research combined physiological observation with psychoanalytic interviews with patients with petit mal. I became joint editor of the *Association of Psychoanalytic Psychotherapists Newsletter in the National Health Service* and originated an experiential Masters course on Caring for the Bereaved and the Dying at Middlesex University and the Tavistock Clinic. I published widely on a variety of topics, but my research principally concerned the relationship of mental events to psychosociological phenomena, including hypnosis and trauma, epilepsy, sleep patterns in infants, intracranial bruits and attention and inattention in neurophysiology. My psychoanalytic training was at the Institute of Psychoanalysis in London, where I was supervised by Dr Hannah Segal and Dr Wilfrid Bion, who inspired much of my thinking about the approach to seriously ill patients.

Although the material for this book derives solely from the work I did with cancer patients, its conception and production is the result of a collaboration with Jane Desmarais, who has, to use a medical simile, helped the birth of this book very much as a midwife helps to deliver a baby. She teaches in the Department of English and Comparative Literature at Goldsmiths College, University of London, and is an editor of psychoanalytical literature, her most recent collaboration being on the subject of eating disorders and two volumes entitled *The Generosity of Acceptance*, edited with Gianna Williams, Paul Williams and Kent Ravenscroft (Karnac, 2003). She has written on anorexia and passive resistance in Hermann Melville's 1853 tale, *Bartleby*, and is the author and editor of other books, essays and articles on the literature and visual arts of the nineteenth century. Jane Desmarais enabled my original conception of the book to be realised in assembling it from my personal archive of clinical notes and papers, so that a selection of these could be put into book order.

Every effort has been made to protect the confidentiality of individual patients and to convey in plain language some of the issues surrounding cancer care. The clinical vignettes throughout the book are usually brief and are occasionally more detailed. Their inclusion is not to be compared with material that might be presented in a medical text with a pattern of symptoms and a prognosis. Rather, they are intended to illustrate the dynamic process of listening and talking to the dying and the courage of many of these patients in their attempts to help others.

Most of the psychoanalytic–psychotherapeutic work described in this book was done in London, principally at the Institute of Oncology at the Royal Marsden Hospital, but also at the Institute of Obstetrics and Gynaecology at the Hammersmith Hospital and the Institute of Otolaryngology at the Throat, Nose and Ear Hospital. The Institute of Oncology specialises in the treatment and investigation of cancer of all types in patients of all ages, and it provided a wealth and range of material. There, I evolved a philosophy of patient care in the course of speaking to children, adolescents and adults with cancer in the hospital setting. The accounts of talking with these patients given here illustrate, for the first time in the cancer literature, how the special kind of attention and care afforded by psychoanalytic psychotherapy can bring to dying people not just a sense of dignity and worth, but can also empower them to take control of various physical aspects of their condition.

In a letter written in 1787 to his father, Mozart wrote:

> Since death, when we come to consider it closely, is the true goal of our existence, I have formed during the last few years such close relationships with this best and truest friend of mankind, that his image is not only no longer terrifying to me but actually soothing and consoling. I thank God for allowing me to understand that the fact of death is the key which unlocks the door to true happiness. I never lie down at night without reflecting that young though I am I may not live to see another day.[1]

So many patients are vulnerable and helpless in the face of serious and terminal illness, and 'the fact of death' remains something banished to the corners of most people's minds. So many, too, in the 'helping professions' are themselves afraid of death and this fear inhibits them from recognising the courage and purpose of some of their patients. They may avoid those patients who are unafraid of their condition, and project their own anxiety and fears about death into those for whom they care. The doctor or nurse who can help the individual patient to suffer rather than suffer from their disease is a rare figure in our hospitals.

The medical doctor examines the body and, from the combination of symptoms and signs, diagnoses the condition and its relationship to symptoms of other known diseases. In this process of medical diagnosis, the doctor moves away from consideration of the particular individual to the general processes of the disease. In short, the doctor is not concerned with how the individual feels or thinks but how the disease performs. With cancer patients, on whom the disease makes a devastating psychological impression, physical treatment and palliation can only do so much.

As a psychiatrist with training and experience in psychoanalytic psychotherapy, I approached all my patients as individuals. I had no preconceptions: I had never met them before, and I knew nothing about their histories. I would treat any patient suffering from cancer; no patient was rejected because of their age, condition, or ability to pay. I introduced myself in hospital, often at their bedside, and an arrangement was set up for as long as it would be possible. Each time I and the patient met – if possible, on alternate days – I would be there for approximately an hour. I asked the patients to say whatever came into their mind, and treated everything they said with the strictest confidentiality. Although the content of our sessions was not recorded in the hospital notes or in letters to other doctors, I kept careful written records of my meetings with these patients. This material forms the basis of this book.

Psychotherapy and the Treatment of Cancer Patients: Bearing Cancer in Mind is a reflection on the most important aspects of my psychotherapeutic work with cancer patients, and it underlines the multiplicity of psychological effects of cancer on the individual – the complex impact it has, for example, on families and society in general. Most significantly, it describes the need for a multidisciplinary, complementary, integrated treatment within the hospital context, that is, a care of these patients which pays attention to the mental anguish as well as the physical distress caused by the disease. This book advocates a more holistic approach to the cancer patient and suggests ways in which more expert attention might be provided through awareness, training and resources.

The most important and radical feature of *Psychotherapy and the Treatment of Cancer Patients: Bearing Cancer in Mind* is the innovation of applying the psychoanalytic–psychotherapeutic approach within the hospital context to help individuals cope with cancer. This challenges the existing orthodoxies about palliative care and points to ways in which the principles and methods of psychoanalysis can be applied successfully within the hospital context. Most people would agree that cancer patients deserve psychotherapeutic attention, but too few believe that psychoanalysis, which in its classical form is inaccessible to the 'ordinary' person, can be made to happen within a busy hospital. Psychoanalysis is not for the people still; it is for those who can afford to train or undergo analysis, and that leads to some uncomfortable inequities. If psychoanalysis is for the general public good (and recent research shows that it produces tangible and positive results in certain groups of people), then it should cast its net wider. In medicine, the aim has always been, and still is, to find the people that need the help, and it was a truism of those who campaigned for the National Health Service that 'charity was no substitute for organised justice'.[2] If psychoanalytic provision is to be more diverse and just, then there must be a concerted effort – particularly by the major training institutes – to move beyond the narrow demographics of current provision. The religiosity that characterises psychoanalysis and training institutes must cease to enable normal training procedures to be implemented. If this does not happen there can be no integration of psychoanalysis within National Health Service hospitals treating all patients without the constraint of fees for service.

The monastic self-importance of certain clinics and psychoanalytical institutions in addressing their public role and image have contributed much to the stereotypical image of analysis as elitist, exclusive, exploitative and, perhaps most damagingly, self-proving.[3] This has resulted in a confused public perception about what psychoanalysis really is. For modern psychoanalysis, detached from and unembraced by the majority, the issues of class, accessibility and accountability are of great concern, and although much has been done to improve the levels of individual support and professional duty, much more is still to be done.

There are many books and articles on the topic of cancer care, usually with an emphasis on a particular aspect, such as 'palliative care', or on a particular psychological approach, such as Cognitive Behavioural Therapy.[4] There is very little generally published, however, on what has been termed psycho-oncology, that is, the study of the emotional responses of cancer patients and their families and the effect of psychological, behavioural and social factors on rates of morbidity and mortality.[5] As recently as 1999, in the *Psychiatric Bulletin*, Charles Montgomery recommended the incorporation of psychosocial interventions within hospitals, but the necessary research and training in this field is still being developed.

The application of psychoanalytical ideas to therapeutic work with cancer patients is virtually non-existent, and that which is accessible is not up-to-date and tends to concentrate on the counter-transferential experience of the analyst.[6] Since the 1970s, when the mental health of cancer patients became an issue, the emphasis has tended to be on the prevention of distress and the enhancement of ways of coping with the trauma of cancer. Some notable work has been published in the United States on this subject. Particularly noteworthy is work by B. Keizer, who recounts individual stories of those dying from cancer (*Dancing with Mister D: Notes on Life and Death*, Doubleday, 1997), and by Lawrence Le Shan, who is the only one to describe dynamic-type psychotherapy work with cancer patients (*You Can Fight for Your Life*, Evans & Co., 1977 and *Cancer as a Turning-Point*, Dutton, 1989).

Each chapter of *Psychotherapy and the Treatment of Cancer Patients: Bearing Cancer in Mind* deals with a different aspect of work with cancer patients. In Chapter 1, 'In the front line with cancer', the analogy between the suffering of soldiers and cancer patients is made to suggest the similar ways in which these individuals are marginalised and stigmatised by what has been termed 'attrition of the self'. This chapter describes how the individual's sense of life, including their delusions about life, is stripped away on receiving the diagnosis of cancer. This event constitutes, in effect, a 'catastrophe', an event producing the subversion of the order or system of things, and dramatically changing the patient's inner world view. This first chapter proposes that psychological forces be taken into account in the physical treatment of cancer, and rather like the innovative approach of W.H. Rivers after the First World War, it advocates a perspective of the sufferers as people who are not victims but stoics in the face of death.

Chapter 2, 'Cancer and the psychotherapeutic endeavour' differentiates the practice of psychotherapy with cancer patients in a hospital environment from the practice of private consultation, whereby the patient pays a fee and lies on the couch for fifty minutes. The psychotherapy arrangement described in the hospital contrasts with many of the general hospital procedures. The time allotted for the meeting between the therapist and the patient is greater than any other meeting between doctor and patient. It is private and confidential, even at the bedside, and amid the hurly-burly of the ward, the staff show their respect for the process by protecting the patient and therapist from interruptions.

In the next chapter, 'The impact of cancer on hospital relationships', the implications of cancer for relationships between staff and patients and the world beyond hospital are considered. When an individual is diagnosed with cancer he or she tends to lose their established sense of self in the community and in the hospital world becomes a cipher. This kind of marginalisation makes patients extremely vulnerable to despair and their relationships, both internal and external to the hospital environment, can be seriously undermined as a consequence.

Chapter 4 deals specifically with cancer in different areas of the body and mind, and describes the different forms of cancer and the effect they have on different parts of the body and the individual's conception of his or her own body. The relationship between mental states and an individual's self-perception is explored and the effect of various factors is discussed, including the effect of age on the reaction to cancer, the contrast between cancers of the head and neck region and cancers inside and away from the head in the body. The diagnosis of cancers of the blood or lymphatic system, which affect the life of the patient over a long period of time, are compared to 'solid' cancers, and a lengthy concluding section is devoted to the effects of gynaecological cancer.

Physical pain and pain relief are important issues in relation to cancer and can be the main and only topics for discussion between doctor and patient. There is usually little else that can be said without unease about the condition. Through psychoanalytic psychotherapy, the relief of mental pain may result in a diminished concern with physical pain or discomfort. In 'Mind-bending pain', I examine the psychological territory of pain perception and apperception and different reactions to pain from the point of view of both the patient and the oncologist. Chapter 6 'Dread and trauma – on being told the truth' is about the function and role of truth in dealing with cancer patients. It is based on my paper, 'The Ethics of Telling the Patient' (first published in the *Journal of Medical Ethics* in 1982), and it describes how the timing and the circumstances make a profound difference to the recipient of bad news.

The book closes with two chapters that draw on my experience working in the National Health Service and the particular issues that arise with working with patients in a 'general' hospital. Chapter 7, 'Psycho-analytic psychotherapy in the NHS "general" hospital' focuses on the usefulness of psychotherapeutic interventions in three London teaching hospitals, and in the concluding Chapter 8, 'Examining group processes in hospital', working with and amidst cancer patients is shown to affect the carers in unexpected ways. There is a high failure rate in medical terms. The gratification of a 'cure' is rare, and an underlying sense of futility in applying different treatments can produce diversionary rivalries and a preoccupation with statistics. As described in Chapter 3, the dying person in a general hospital becomes unimportant. There is a tendency to isolate human beings who are going to die, yet there is a fantasy of loneliness and abandonment associated with death. The discourse with a very ill person has to have a special quality; it cannot be 'ordinary', and often the nurse and the doctor do not know how to make it extra-ordinary at an extraordinary time. This last chapter examines the special discourse between patient and medical professionals and argues for the institution of special training which would underline its value in a context constrained by cancer.

Psychotherapy and the Treatment of Cancer Patients: Bearing Cancer in Mind offers a radically different approach to people who are seriously ill. It is a book for everybody who is concerned about how seriously ill patients with cancer and other serious conditions are neglected psychologically. Cancer impinges in some way on all our lives. Recent research has shown that over 230,000 people are diagnosed with cancer each year, and a quarter of all deaths are due to cancer.[7] Traditionally, in regard to cancer, society has been an ostrich with its head in the sand. Cancer has been the province of physical medicine and it has been left up to physicians to make the decisions. I argue that patients should be approached in complementary ways as victims of a personal disaster, a catastrophe that has wreaked havoc on their lives, which has isolated them from 'well' others. They should never be left alone; this most important period of an individual's life is when the attention of others is most needed. This is the psychotherapeutic endeavour.

Notes

1   *The Letters of Wolfgang Amadeus Mozart*, translated from the collection of Ludwig Nohl by Lady Wallace, Boston, 1864, pp. 221–222.
2   This is from Aneurin Bevan's last speech on the National Health Service, delivered to the House of Commons in 1958.
3   See César Garza-Guerrero's polemical article, 'Reorganisational and Educational Demands of Psychoanalytic Training Today: Our Long and Marasmic Night of One Century', *International Journal of Psychoanalysis*, 85 (2004), 3–25.
4   For example, see John Ellershaw and Chris Ward, 'Care of the Dying Patient: The Last Hours or Days of Life', *British Medical Journal*, 326 (2003), 30–34.
5   There is, of course, *Psycho-Oncology*, co-edited by Jimmie Holland and Maggie Watson, but this is an academic journal with a specialist readership.
6   See Florence Joseph, 'Transference and Countertransference in the Case of a Dying Patient', in *Psychoanalytic Review*, 49 (1962), 21–34.
7   See Zosia Kmietowicz's piece in the 'News' section of the *British Medical Journal*, 27 March 2004 entitled 'Palliative care services should have higher priorities, says NICE'.

Chapter 1

In the front line with cancer

The discovery of cancer plunges the normal individual into the abnormal world of the hospital. It can be a dehumanising process: individuality is lost. Dresses and suits are replaced by simple night attire, dressing gowns are nondescript; individuals become 'patients' with a number more important than their name. They are disempowered and beholden to all 'non-patients'. In becoming ill, they enter hospital, a world apart, where no one really listens to anything but answers to stylised questions. What cancer patients suffer from first of all is a kind of shell shock brought about by the diagnosis and the dislocation from ordinary life. Cancer engenders considerable trauma.

In this chapter, I compare working with cancer patients to being in the line of action in a war situation, and having cancer to having the symptoms of shell shock. In the same way that soldiers during the First World War suffered from psychological trauma that went unheeded, I argue that the mental states of cancer patients have been ignored. Psychoanalytic psychotherapy is an important intervention for patients within the hospital context, and in the clinical cases selected in the second part of this chapter there is a transformation in the suffering individual as they begin to talk and to be listened to. Some patients experience a release of creativity whereas others are able to change their way of thinking and show concern for others at the most painful part of their life.

An attrition of the self

The first observations of psychological reactions to trauma were made during the First World War, most notably by W.H.R. Rivers.[1] The conditions that men endured at that time were unprecedented. Rivers found that what he saw in his patients confirmed much of what he had read in Freud, the only person to have made a systematic study of mental processes. In his observations of war trauma, Rivers found that there were confusing moral issues to be considered. What did it mean to get one of these men 'better'? Medically, it was to help them recover their pre-trauma state, but militarily it was to return them to the very conditions that had produced their breakdown. These two aims were in conflict in his mind.

Carl May (1998) quoting from Lord Moran's 1945 'Memoir', describes the soldiers of the 1914–18 war as men who were unafraid of death if it came swiftly and decently, but who were unable to cope when they were hit by random shelling on a huge scale. It was too much for them. They were too passive. May comments:

> Courage, of course remained the normative expectation of the fighting man. However, the way in which courage itself was conceptualised changed: it shifted from episodic physical heroism to stoical endurance and adjustment to powerlessness. The individual soldier on the Western Front often appeared to have little effect on the outcome of anything; his actions only became meaningful in relation to membership of a group that suffered annihilation in the most random way. Individuals faced the prospect of weeks and months of physical and psychological hardship followed by a random, meaningless and repulsive death.[2]

It was Elliot Smith, however, Professor of Anatomy and Dean of Medicine at Manchester University, who argued in the *Lancet* in 1916 that the real trauma of war was 'psychical not physical'. He called it 'war strain' not 'shell shock' and he argued that 'it was due to "an attrition of the self"', suffered by exposure to terrible anxiety and reminders of their own peril by the deaths of those around them'.[3] He realised that individuals in war were exposed to unprecedented conditions, and that the war precipitated great numbers of people from their everyday lives into another world; a world of obscene mutilations and death. This could apply to a ward of cancer patients, particularly the 'terminal ward'. Cancer patients also feel themselves to be helpless victims of a random process ending in death, and when I began working in the hospital and my colleagues referred patients who were very distressed, I wondered, like Rivers, what was expected of me. Was I to make patients 'better'? What was 'better'? If they became cheerful and happy despite their physical state, was this successful treatment? How was I, as both a physician and psychotherapist, to help? How was I to bring the two approaches together to good effect?

Cancer treatment by chemotherapy (ironically one of the first chemotherapy agents was mustard gas used in the First World War) and surgery has changed the course of the disease and lengthened the survival time of patients. This treatment produces its own stresses and strains and the individual has no guarantee of cure. Descriptions of 'shell shock' resonate here; they could apply to the young men with cancer, who, in profound despair, become mute and unresponsive. In his 'Memoir', Lord Moran described a soldier who became mute and apathetic and later shot himself. Moran admits that initially he gave it little attention. This soldier was clearly not afraid of death, but he could not face the trenches, and worse, the accusations of cowardice and the reproaches of his fellow sufferers in the trenches. Moran describes his own reaction to this man's suicide in a way that is uncomprehending (to put it mildly) of the soldier's state of mind.[4] He thought it was a condition of the poorer, inferior classes and therefore not a condition of officers! Later, when he experiences a close bombardment, he becomes more sympathetic to the suffering of the soldiers. Experiencing the 'corrosion' of the battlefield at first hand, *he* suffers all the symptoms of 'shell shock'!

The 'shell shock' of cancer

The questions that beset Rivers concerning 'treatment' of shell shock are applicable to the treatment of cancer patients. Many that I saw were in pain that was distressing and could not be relieved. In many cases, the patient's condition was deteriorating and treatment had ceased; sometimes a token course of treatment was initiated with no real hope of its effectiveness. I was in a different position to Rivers in that I was with the patients in the 'front line' and there was no way of avoiding the pounding, from the disease, the treatment and the disability, which the patient suffered.

Ubiquitous phantasies about death and dying inform many of the attitudes in hospitals towards the dying patient. Isolation is a universally feared option; and yet the practice is to isolate dying patients and then hide them from view using single side-rooms and screened-off beds. Our own attitudes towards death affect the way in which others are cared for. In 1915, Freud wrote about the difficulty of imagining our own death in 'Thoughts for the Times on War and Death'. He described war as being:

> . . . far from straightforward. To any one who listened to us we were of course prepared to maintain that death was the necessary outcome of life, that everyone owes nature a death and must expect to pay the debt – in short that death was natural, undeniable and unavoidable.

In reality, we are accustomed to behave as if it were otherwise. We show an unmistakable tendency to put death on one side, to eliminate it from life. It is indeed impossible to imagine our own death; and whenever we attempt to do so we can perceive that we are in fact still present as spectators. Hence the psychoanalytic school could venture on the assertion that at bottom no one believes in his own death, or, to put the same thing in another way, that in the unconscious every one of us is convinced of his own immortality.[5]

Eighty years after the First World War a review took place of all instances in that war when soldiers were shot for cowardice. They were perceived as being brave men paralysed by the inner conflict between group obligations and an uncontrollable aversion to war conditions. Through his work with victims of shell shock, Rivers challenged the prevailing view of soldiers with mutism, which saw them as individuals consciously refusing to speak. Instead, he took a more compassionate stance, maintaining that that they were victims of an inner conflict produced by the terrible conditions.

Attention to psychological trauma in the general hospital

The influence of psychological forces on physical processes in a general hospital is generally unacknowledged because no one understands them or how to use them in the treatment of the *whole* patient. There is also an aversion to considering 'mind processes'. People specialised in their knowledge of physical processes stay with what they know: which is also what they can control. My armamentarium of 'just words' was unimpressive in comparison to the resources of a physician or anaesthetist for treating pain and the high-tech world of a modern hospital with its 'scans', magnetic resonance imaging, computer tomography, and other equipment (mainly for diagnosis and X-ray machines for radiotherapy). But this leaves out of the account the healing properties of talking and listening, and the untapped power of the mind for denying, or modifying, the effects of sensory input to the body. The diagnosis of cancer itself produces physiological and psychological pain, it produces pain and shock, sometimes experienced simultaneously.

In the case of trauma caused by cancer, the relationship between patient and doctor in psychoanalytic psychotherapy occurs immediately and is from a very early and primitive relationship, that is, it is a relationship stripped of defences and pretences, and resembles very early relationships between, say a parent and a child. It is important to realise that it comes into being because of the traumatic situation and not because of any special features in the doctor or nurse. After the patient has been told that they have cancer their doctors become empowered and have a responsibility to act with care. Both patient and doctor are vulnerable; the doctor from feelings of omnipotence and the patient from extreme passivity. The significance of pain for the patient, how it is perceived, is rarely discussed. The patient might ask is this pain going to be for the rest of my life? What is pain relief going to do to my sense of the world? The answers to these questions can directly influence vital functions, but in many cases, the patient does not get to ask questions.

The task of trying to understand and help the patient understand unconscious thought processes is the province of the psychoanalyst and it is that form of enquiry and procedure, this book aims to show, which is most appropriate for the alleviation of deep mental pain and suffering.

The following accounts are a selection from the hundreds of patients I saw when I was a psychiatric consultant working mainly at the Royal Marsden Hospital and also, but much less frequently, at the Royal National Ear, Nose and Throat Hospital and the Institute of Obstetrics and Gynaecology at the Hammersmith Hospital in London.

The psychotherapy 'process'

The psychotherapy 'process' is with each patient a 'pure' research project. Neither the patient nor the therapist knows what we will discover following the truth. It is not 'invention' in the sense of having an objective; which in these circumstances could be to relieve anxiety, reduce fear, produce an 'acceptance' of death. There are no prior formulations of aims and no promises. The psychological situation is entirely different when surgery and other measures have eliminated cancer. These patients have difficulties, not because of pain and imminent death, but because life now has many things missing from it that make it enjoyable. Patients feeling quite well can discover they have cancer and then feel unwell after treatment. The treatment produces changes that can devastate their life. For example, some men with cancer of the testicle feel castrated, and women made infertile by treatment for cancer of the genitalia may feel 'de-feminised'. The surgical removal of cancer in the head and neck region may result in the loss of the larynx, oesophagus or tongue, removing the normal means of communication. All these constitute, in effect, a subversion of the order of things for the patient, whose world is turned upside down.

Without a voice

Passing the ward office on my round one day, the nurse on duty said 'Could you see the patient, a nice lady, in the second bed before she goes?' There was no suggestion that she was 'difficult', 'neurotic' or depressed. By the bed stood a fit, smartly dressed woman with her case closed ready to go . . . She was in striking contrast to all the other patients on this large ward who looked unwell, as they lay quiet and pale in their beds. Mouthing the words she responded to my greeting, and I knew why I was there and what had happened to her. The cancer had gone and so had her larynx. I later realised that the cancer had been in the oesophagus and both larynx and oesophagus had had to be removed. Her life and the capacity to enjoy life had gone with them.

She spoke with the faintest of whispers shaping exhaled breath into words. She had no voice, and unlike the laryngectomy patients who use oesophageal speech, she could not swallow air. Eliminating cancer in the sites of the oesophagus and larynx involves the removal of the structure that contains it. Life without these structures is unimaginable and the experience traumatic. She had not fully appreciated the consequences of the operation. When she had learned she had cancer, her prime concern was the preservation of her life, not how she would live that life.

When she was working, she spent her time talking to her clients on the telephone. Without audible speech she was ruined. Instead of her oesophagus, she now had a piece of large bowel running under the skin of her chest. Loud gurgling noises issued from her misshapen chest, and she would awaken to find bile stains on her pillow. She felt she could not share her bed with anyone. She could not socialise and she could not make love. She had suffered a loss of life, her way of life. She felt she could not engage in psychotherapy until she found a way of speaking with greater facility. I thought that psychotherapy using writing to communicate would be valuable; it could be a way of 'brain storming' to find ways of living, with fulfilment. Nothing in her life had prepared her for this eventuality. She felt too hopeless at this point, however, to consider that anything could help her.

Learning to take charge

One young woman when she first developed breast cancer had no doubt that she could control and cope with it as she had with everything else in her life. She felt that she could cope with any eventuality in her life; up until she was diagnosed with cancer, nothing had shaken this belief. She had a mastectomy and without drawing breath, as it were, she continued her very busy professional and domestic life. After two years the cancer recurred and it was then that her fantasy that she could cope with anything was exposed. She was the lynchpin of the family, looking after her husband, two young children and two elderly relatives at the same time as working full time in her profession. She was devastated when the cancer recurred because she believed that she had 'defeated' it. She said 'It has come back. I have failed! I am going to die!' She felt that there was no point in speaking. She was the last person her 'dependants' would have expected to collapse; previously able to conquer any difficulty, she was now completely powerless. I suggested psychotherapy as a way of exploring her situation. She could not conceive of how anyone could help her situation, nevertheless she accepted my offer. She left hospital and came weekly to see me for several months for psychotherapy. She quickly realised that she was the victim of her own thinking. She had to believe again that she could cope with and control everything in her life. The work we did was constructive and engaging. She acquired insight rapidly and she knew we would carry on for as long as possible. There was no anxiety or fear and during one of our last meetings she said, referring to her own experience of psychotherapy 'I would not have missed this for anything!' She had changed her views of all her relationships and she felt liberated from her burdens placed upon her by internal demands. Something good and positive had resulted from her illness. She valued the release from the internal straight jacket. She was in charge of herself, integrated and independent.

This woman's response was mirrored in the interviews I had with old soldiers from the 1914–18 war about their experiences. Grim though they were, they would say: 'I would not have missed it for anything!' They had endured unimaginable conditions and found that they could survive. They would also say that they experienced a comradeship in the trenches which was incomparable. This too was something undreamed of, and now treasured. Many patients with cancer had comparable experiences; laryngectomy patients formed spirited groups that met long after they left hospital. Some went through terrible experiences with a partner, discovering in so doing, an awareness of a deep affection between them or a love greater and more profound than anything that had existed before. In some instances psychotherapy was the catalyst for a relationship to develop in this way. Where a close relationship did not exist before admission, I became the needed companion as the patient ran the gauntlet of diagnosis, treatment and disability.

Losing everything

The words 'don't get pregnant!' destroyed the dream of a young woman with breast cancer. She was at the hospital to hear the results of a biopsy of a lump found in her breast. Her elderly parents both had cancer but being young, she did not expect cancer. Her husband's response was wild and desperate, he urged her to take LSD because he thought that with the mind changes it engendered the cancer would be defeated. She was sceptical and said that she wanted to discuss this with a psychiatrist. When we met for the first time, it appeared that she had ignored her husband's suggestion. Nevertheless, she did want help and wanted to know the differences between 'psychotherapy', 'psychoanalysis' and the 'consultations' she had experienced with various doctors. She accepted my offer of thrice-weekly sessions outside the hospital in my consulting rooms. Her parents waiting in outpatients indicated as I passed how pleased and relieved they were at this decision. I thought of their terrible cruel dilemma in which they could not comfort their daughter or offer solace. Her cancer was growing rapidly and theirs was slow; she was going to die before them. They knew about psychoanalysis and seemed relieved to know that she was going to be involved in a process that addressed her deepest feelings and enabled the free expression of them. They knew it was not about treatment or reassurance, which was all that she had been able to talk about to the doctors. She could not, it seemed, have an exchange that was worthwhile with her husband. He was frantic and initially blamed his wife for her condition because she had not taken up the suggestions that he had made, which included her taking LSD and practising visualisation techniques. I offered to see her for psychotherapy and said that I felt that this would be exploratory; I did not know how it would develop. I thought that it was the best thing we could do. She decided to go ahead with this though it had nothing to do with her original request. I offered her sessions three times a week with no time limit on my obligation to see her, for as long as needed.

For this young woman, the feelings of loss were permanent, and in the sessions she was able to articulate these through dreams she had had. One of the first dreams she recounted was about losses, the most important loss due to the cancer being losing the freedom to conceive, to have a baby. In the dream she had a baby but feels very selfish as she is going to die leaving her husband to care for it. As well as loss, the session revealed her deep resentment about having cancer. This came out in an association of ideas. In one session she recalled her feelings when her brother was born. She was eighteen months old and she resented the interference it caused in her life just as she did the cancer.

Being beyond hope

A 62-year-old unmarried woman complained of tiredness and depression despite assurances that cancer of the bowel treated twelve months previously had ceased to grow. She was not convinced by the doctor who told her that she was fortunate to have an extended lease of life. She was sure there was something wrong and she was deteriorating. She lived on her own and during her stay in hospital a woman whom she had rescued and cared for as a child came to England to look after her, to repay her debt to her. She did not respond with gratitude or friendliness to this devoted woman. She refused to see her religious relatives because she alleged they would say she got cancer because she was not religious. A religious charity group sent visitors and she rejected them, assuming that they came out of duty. She wanted genuine friendship. She was convinced that she was deteriorating because of the cancer and would become dependent on others. She said that no one had given her a direct answer to her question as to the cause of the weakness in her legs. In the past, she had been stoical about pain and death. She left hospital and returned some months later still complaining that she was growing weak. She told me of a dream that she had. It was long and appeared to her to have gone on into the day so that she did not know what day it was. In the dream she goes to Australia, a place she had never been to. It was different from anything she had seen before with wide-open spaces. She realised that she had always been afraid of dying and going to another place.

Two devoted friends, including the one she had cared for as a child, stayed with her constantly and they described how she went to sleep one night and at 6 a.m. died without awakening. Her friends said that at the end she had given up hope and seemed to be willing herself to die. Physically she had not changed. She was a lonely woman saying that she wanted friends and companionship but rejecting all attempts to engage her. It seemed that she felt condemned after the first drug prescribed by the oncologist. She was convinced that the cancer was going to kill her. She felt that no matter what people said they had really given up hope for her. In her internal world, there were figures who regarded her as beyond hope. She had no place in their minds and hearts. This was her reality.

Writing for life

In a selection of the letters of servicemen facing death in the 1939–45 war we find endless independent statements of principle and evaluations of the truth.[6] They are often eloquent and expressive in describing intimate feelings; many knowing as they write that they are unlikely to see their respondent again. Dr Johnson's famous comment comes to mind here. In answer to someone who had said that a Dr Dodd could not have written 'The Convict's Address to his unhappy Brethren' because it contained a great deal more force of mind in it than anything known to be his, Dr Johnson responded, 'Why should you think so? Depend upon it Sir, when a man knows he is to be hanged in a fortnight, it concentrates his mind wonderfully'.[7] All the soldiers writing hoped that their life would contribute to making the world a better place for others. Many cancer patients also sought this reassurance for themselves; hoping that they had been worthwhile. The soldiers were not pugnacious or angry with the 'enemy', as patients do not, in general, rage against the disease. After the war, one woman auxiliary who was mentioned said that in normal circumstances she would not have written so frankly. The letters of servicemen included letters by lovers, siblings, parents to children, and children, sons and daughters, to their parents. The young soldiers seemed to understand their parents' pain in thinking about death and death's imminence. Through the letters, the soldiers were establishing their place in another person's mind. It is the most important thing in their life. Their minds were full of people to whom they were precious. The people in their inner world were vital, alive and thinking. This was apparent in the way they wrote because they wrote as if they were speaking to the person.

Feeling contained

The many patients that I was with before they died were also thinking about putting thoughts together and speaking about their lives and relationships. They were speaking directly to a stranger but, after the introductory exchange, it seemed as if we were not speaking as strangers to one another. I was entrusted with the last thoughts of hundreds of people with cancer during the most demanding period of their life. I appeared to function, to use the psychoanalyst Wilfrid Bion's term, as a 'container' for their anxiety. By this I mean that I contained and thereby limited their anxiety, responding with an unanxious, calm concern. In Bion's terms, there was a 'thinker' in the therapeutic relationship who put thoughts together. When a patient and I began to work together, a 'thinker' also came into being. This experience occurred many times and could be psychologically quite dramatic, although the physical status remained unaltered. This is analogous to the situation when for example a small child falls and hurts itself and crying runs to its mother. She 'kisses it better', but physically nothing has changed. She takes the load of pain and distress and returns it with the pain removed, as warmth, and comforting calm, the kiss and hug representing acceptance of the weal and woe of the baby. The mother perceives the pain as a transient phenomenon, with a beginning and an end, but the baby experiences pain without a beginning or end until it is contained, and limited. The contained is past, and there is therefore a 'future' perceived without pain.

The presence of serious illness has the same effect. All constructive thought is displaced by unremitting pain and the mental pain following wounding news of treatment failure produces an 'end of the world' feeling. Very ill patients who feel 'contained', however, can come to feel that they have a future. The feeling of not being contained, and worse, being unacceptable to others, is dreaded more than anything and leads to a decline in vitality and death.

The difficulty in relinquishing control

A 40-year-old man receiving chemotherapy for an acute form of leukaemia as an outpatient appeared to be distressed but his wife seemed unperturbed. The nurses wondered if his wife was unaware of the diagnosis. She described how three weeks previously the illness had come as a shock to them all and he became a hospital inpatient. They wanted to be together at the first meeting with the doctor who I was supervising. After the doctor introduced herself, explaining her role, she invited them to freely express their feelings. The following exchanges occurred.

The patient said, 'I am very pleased to see you. I have to be very positive. I have read some book on being positive. You know what I mean . . . "visualisation". I have to see the chemotherapy as drugs that are killing off the bad cells. I must think in this way about the drugs.' As he spoke, overwhelmed with his feelings, he burst into tears. He repeated the claim that he wanted to be positive several times. He appeared to be talking to himself as if trying to convince himself. He said 'I see this problem, the complication, as a blip in my progress.'

He produced a book in which he had written down all the drugs, his temperatures and other test results. He said, 'It helps me to write it all down.' This appeared to be an obsessive response to feeling helpless. 'I need to know everything. I am getting more positive.' He then said how lucky he was, and then looking at his wife – how lucky he was to have children. He exclaimed, 'I want you to teach me to be positive!' The doctor's reaction to this patient was to advise that perhaps the patient should see a behavioural therapist.

Later, the doctor returned to find the patient lying on his bed holding his head and looking very distressed. He reiterated that he wanted to be told how to be positive. The doctor responded by saying, 'When you told me about how you were facing your chemotherapy it felt to me to be a very positive way of looking at it, but you seem to be to be telling yourself over and over again that you must be positive; it does not feel to me as though you are really experiencing it. It is as though you have to be very positive, as the opposite will be completely negative. Perhaps one can have a mixture of both sorts of feelings. A kind of balance – somewhere in the middle.' There was a marked change and he stopped crying and took his hand off his head. He then described how he had moved to a new job, which he enjoyed, and where he felt valued when 'everything turned upside down . . . my whole life. Life was a shattering explosion. Everything was all right until three weeks ago. I suppose trying to be positive is really about denial. Felt fine, then the headaches . . . a blood test and then you hear that you have leukaemia and if it is not treated you have six to eight weeks left to live! One thing after the other I felt swamped. I felt confused. The fear I have of being out of control! I am only human!'

This case illustrates an obsessional efficient individual, used to being in control, shattered by something that he cannot control. Temporarily, this usually pragmatic man clutches at straws, magical straws. In hospital he has this singular experience of being with an open-minded doctor, trained to listen, and the patient's anxieties are contained. When his communications are returned with a different perspective he feels some anxiety removed; 'It has helped to talk', he declared at the end of the session. 'I have to look at my life. The real treasures are my wife and kids. I want to spend time with them. It has been a pleasure talking to you.' The transformation as he counts his blessings are very moving for both the patient and the doctor.

The effect of cancer on the successful individual

The acquisition of power in many professions may be deemed a success in itself, or 'success' may bring with it power; either way it may corrupt the individual. The individual comes to believe that their position and success in life is entirely due to their own perspicacity and accidents and illnesses overtake lesser beings. It is necessary to understand this process to understand the reactions of apparently controlled and successful individuals to cancer. The conscientious workaholic accountant, for example, is efficient and works long hours to the advantage of the clients, so is the 'successful' manager/organiser. The immediate and profound collapse into despair when such a person develops cancer can come as a terrible shock.

Patients with previously untreated psychological neuroses sometimes found unexpected help in the first psychotherapeutic intervention offered as part of their cancer treatment. These individuals had not sought psychological help before they became cancer patients because of their professional status and the stigma attaching to someone of their position consulting a psychiatrist. None of the patients that I met had considered psychotherapy. Cancer brought them into contact with psychotherapy without the stigma.

Outward efficiency: inward terror

When the head of a successful academic institution learned that he had Hodgkin's disease (disease of the lymph glands) he asked if he could see a psychiatrist. At our first meeting, the patient, without any reference to his illness, immediately plunged into a description of his obsessional rituals. No one in his family knew about them and the rituals had multiplied to such an extent that he feared that he would shortly be unable to get to work. They were more time-consuming and he could not get to his work before midday. He felt something terrible would happen if he did not perform them. The outward appearance was of an efficient executive but inwardly he was terrified of the consequences of not performing his rituals. My first session with him was his first contact with a psychiatrist or psychotherapist. I could only assume that he had not consulted anyone before because he was ashamed or thought that it might jeopardise his career. The physical disease gave him the opportunity to try to achieve some control and under-standing of his condition without publicity. In other circumstances, it would take much longer and be very difficult to initiate psychotherapy. The sense of relief from his obsession was profound and he appeared unconcerned by the cancer.

The humbling of a senior doctor

A senior doctor who was not a clinician but worked in a laboratory came to see me because of his anxiety and various physical complaints that he suspected as being due to secondary cancer. He was concerned at the possibility that he could have a recurrence in his stomach. He accepted that there was no evidence of this. He had been prescribed an antidepressant but he had not liked the side effects; he had also taken Valium, which he said gave him temporary relief but after the side effects wore off he was worse that he was before. He was almost petulant, saying that he had been depressed in the past but had always been able to get over it himself. At the first meeting he reiterated his belief that he had three physical symptoms – loss of appetite, pain in his abdomen and lassitude – and these were causing his mood of depression. Such was the pressure that he kept repeating his hypothesis and did not appear to listen to what I said. He could not accept my alternative. He felt that his was a rational explanation. He said it was a mystery to him but he did not accept any alternative explanation. At our next meeting, he spent the first forty-five minutes giving me his history with dates and times in meticulous detail. He said that after his first course of radiotherapy, he felt elated and he exercised to test his physical fitness. He had escaped the worst and had not had the symptoms that he had expected from radiotherapy. Then the sickness began and he said 'I was shattered!' He grasped at every straw to reassure himself that one day the symptoms would suddenly disappear, he could not contemplate the possibility that the symptoms would never disappear. He repeated his story of how the physical symptoms preceded the depression and were therefore the cause of it. I was finally able to point out that he seemed to be defending himself against an accusation that his symptoms were emotional in origin. The fact that I, a psychiatrist, had been introduced to him led him to assume that it was thought that his symptoms were 'emotional'. I said that I did not know the origins of his symptoms. Seeing me did not imply that they were emotional in origin. We simply did not know and as he had done everything possible to discover a physical cause he had to accept that he did not know the cause. I was offering to work with him with an open mind. As to the cause of his depression he was trying to make his depression an 'honourable' physical disease that he would term 'a state of depression'.

He finally admitted that he was having a dialogue with himself. One part of him told him that it was in his mind and the other part argued against this. This very experienced scientist set all his scientific knowledge aside when he tried to justify his belief that his depression was physical in origin. Before he became ill he thought people with depression were weak and inferior, hence his strenuous attempts to deny it. His reaction to the radiotherapy indicated that he too was afraid and irrationally he tried to convince himself that he was different from 'ordinary' patients. He was good at his work and obsessional. The obsessionality intensified with the discovery of cancer and exposure of the underlying contempt for depressed psychiatric patients. At the end of the second meeting he was beginning to accept that there might be an alternative interpretation of his depression. He seemed changed, more amenable, warm, modest and likeable. This man abhorred the idea that he had become 'depressed' and was averse to any therapy that was 'psychological'.

Feeling homesick

On another occasion I asked to see a middle-aged man on a ward where most of the patients were receiving palliative care. The nurses had made the request because they had seen him weeping. They had not asked him why he was weeping and no one suggested a reason. They were of the opinion that he did not know that he had cancer. This would have been very unusual in a cancer hospital and it would have been even more surprising if in such a ward he had not asked about his condition. He gave me an ironic account of the last treatment. He said that he knew that it was high-voltage treatment to kill cancer cells but, unfortunately, it had also killed his blood cells because afterwards he had to have a blood transfusion. Because he was a man, he was not supposed to weep and it would embarrass him to mention it. This effectively isolated the patient. He knew he had cancer but no one had discussed the extent of it or the plan of treatment. He told me that he had been weeping because he missed his wife and children, in particular one of his children, who was handicapped. They lived a long way from the hospital and could not visit him. He was at pains to tell me that he had arranged for the family's future and that he had no debts and no outstanding hire-purchase commitments. He was extremely sad because he said that it was just at this time that he should be enjoying life. He was alone and isolated, and there was a failure on the part of the hospital to supply his greatest need, as there was no attempt to bring his children and wife in to see him. The hospital had no social plan for him.

The man was very eager to go home and I advised him that he should go immediately. At this point, he felt homesick and trapped and, despite my advice and his feelings, he was detained at the insistence of the oncologist for three more days of chemotherapy. He died on the last evening.

The power of despair

The rapidity with which despair can overwhelm a patient and lead to death is not realised. Death from destructive physical processes will occur with or without the mental state I have called despair. However, for any individual to die in despair is terrible. It is the cruellest cut of all, and yet preventable. Psychological factors are still not seriously considered when physical disease is diagnosed; the patients' thoughts and feelings are generally the subject of speculation rather than inquiry, the 'speculation' often consisting of the onlooker's own thoughts and phantasies projected on to the patient. This process of 'projective identification'[8] is characterised by the absence of doubt and the presence of certainty. It characterises much professional thinking in medicine. One serious consequence is that nurses and others do not think of asking for psychological help or asking their patients what they have in mind; they think they 'know'. By asking what the patient was thinking, I, by contrast, indicated that I did *not know*, and directed the attention to their 'inner world', the world as they perceived it. That question carried other messages; someone was interested in their personal thoughts and there was the offer of companionship during the exploration.

Talking to be free

As a result of talking and being listened to, patients felt liberated from the entrapment of 'patient-hood'; they were free to talk about anything they chose. This had a salutary effect on thinking; their thoughts were revitalised and more active. The title of one of Wilfrid Bion's books, *A Memoir of The Future*[9] aptly describes one feature of persecutory anxiety experienced by the patient. The patient says, using the future tense, 'I am frightened of what is going to happen to me'. The patient then describes what he or she thinks will, using the future tense, happen. This fantasy of the future is present in their mind, paradoxically, as 'a history of the future'. It establishes a different appreciation of internal reality. The patient realises that they are responding to a fantasy labelled 'future', but they treat it as 'past' and unalterable. A change can be brought about through the intervention of psychoanalytic psychotherapy because it can help the patient transform from feeling persecuted and helpless to feeling empowered to act in the present out of concern about others, a spouse and children for example. The patient can make plans for their future that carry the weight of their authority, rather than medical authority. In most cases, the concern is to put things right, to mend relationships and create love where ill prevails. The opportunity provided by psychoanalytic psycho-therapy to achieve these aims comes from a strong desire to contribute to life and not to accept death in the present.

In this chapter, I have tried to give some sense of the trauma engendered by being diagnosed with cancer and I show, through clinical examples, the range of patients in a hospital context who benefited from psycho-therapeutic intervention. For many, psychotherapy was a liberating experience. In the next chapter, I explain what it means to endeavour to apply psychoanalytic principles to the psychotherapeutic approach to cancer patients. I describe the very significant distinction between what is generally termed 'classical' psychoanalysis (where the patient lies on the couch in a private consulting room) and psychoanalytic psycho-therapy, which is a more flexible derivative approach applied within the hospital context.

Notes

1   See Pat Barker's Regeneration Trilogy: *The Ghost Road*, *The Eye in the Door* and *Regeneration*, Harmondsworth: Penguin, 1993.
2   Carl May, 'Lord Moran's Memoir: Shell Shock and the Pathology of Fear', *Journal of the Royal Society of Medicine*, 91 (1998), 95–100.
3   Elliot G. Smith, 'Shock and the Soldier', *The Lancet*, 2 (1916), 813–817.
4   Elliot G. Smith and T. Pear, *Shell Shock and Its Lessons*, Manchester: Manchester University Press, 1917, p. 2.
5   Sigmund Freud (1915), 'Thoughts for the Times on War and Death', *Standard Edition*, vol. 14, pp. 289–300.
6   See Tamasin Day-Lewis, ed., *Last Letters Home*, London: Macmillan, 1995.
7   From James Boswell's *A Life of Johnson*, ed. R.W. Chapman, Oxford: Oxford University Press, 1904, p. 849.
8   Projective identification is failing to realise that one is identifying processes or features in other people that are really one's own: colloquially, one might say 'seeing one's faults in others' or 'pot calling the kettle black'.
9   Wilfrid Bion, *A Memoir of the Future* [1945], London: Karnac, 1991.

Chapter 2

Cancer and the psychotherapeutic endeavour

Cancer engenders intense social fear and this impacts on patients in hospital, where the majority of doctors and nurses are untrained in dealing with psychological trauma. In this chapter I begin by comparing the approaches of physicians and psychotherapists and argue that by applying the principles of psychoanalysis to psychotherapeutic care, it is possible to relieve some of the mental pain, and indeed in some cases, some of the physical pain of the cancer. Without going into the historical background and theoretical details of psychoanalytic psychotherapy, I outline the ways in which key features of its practice can be adapted to treating patients in hospital.

The specialist hospital

A specialist hospital that focuses upon a particular disease, like cancer, has features that distinguish it from a 'general' hospital. The general hospital admits all types of patient with no restrictions placed on the particular illness from which they suffer. The specialist hospital is exclusive, it provides a facility specifically for patients with diseases, like cancer, and it is usually attached to a research institute. It contains, almost without exception, very ill patients. With regards to cancer, the treatment also makes the sufferer feel ill. Chemotherapy and radiotherapy, for example, are toxic and destructive processes, intended to 'take out' malignant cells and leave others intact. Even though these treatments may not destroy normal healthy cells, the toxic effects can damage some normal cells, or considerably reduce their health, and this can temporarily affect the patient and produce a general debilitating effect. As fast-growing normal cells are vulnerable to the chemicals used to kill cancer cells there may also be a change in personal appearance; most often there is a temporary loss of hair due to chemotherapy. Ablative surgery for cancer of the head and neck may leave its mark on the face and head and even affect speech function and eating. Unlike the general hospital patient, who leaves feeling well, the patient leaving the cancer hospital, however successful the treatment might have been, will feel much worse than when he or she arrived.

Cancer is feared inordinately in our society and its diagnosis is a social stigma that affects both the sufferer's self-perception and the perception of the patient by others. It has common ground with leprosy in that many people are afraid that cancer is 'catching'. One patient went home after treatment for breast cancer to find that her neighbours shut their doors against her and some who had been friends stopped calling on her. She was very angry and astounded at the primitive reaction of those she counted as friends. On the wards of a cancer hospital there was a powerful superstition about the patients with cancer of the head and neck: the staff on the ward would not drink out of clean cups previously used by patients. Many healthy people do not want to associate with someone who has cancer. They are squeamish of the fact and they feel horrified both by its diagnosis in someone else and by the thought that they might one day fall prey to the disease. Many cancer patients feel the horror too, but instead of reacting to the stigmatisation and ostracism with anger and independence, they adopt the stance of the pariah.

Good cancer care

Conceived of as incurable, the diagnosis of cancer is commonly perceived as a death sentence, and it produces a tremendous trauma in the individual sufferer. It is so traumatic to be diagnosed with cancer that it is no surprise that sufferers can become depressed, despairing, even suicidal, and increasingly, physicians are being urged to think about the psychological impact of the disease. In 1995, for example, the Calman–Hine Report advocated 'psychological interventions' as an integral part of 'good' cancer care, and recommended: 'In recognition of the impact of screening, diagnosis and treatment of cancer has on patients, families and their carers, psychosocial aspects of cancer care should be considered at all stages.'[1] What this precisely means or involves, however, was not explicitly explained, and as one critic of the report in the *British Medical Journal* pointed out, the exact nature of 'good' cancer care was not specified.[2] The traditional management of cancer patients at the end of their lives has been to reduce suffering with sedation. Psychiatrists who regard a severe depression in cancer patients as an illness prescribe 'antidepressants', achieving much the same effect as the physician's sedation to suppress pain. In each case there is no conception of psychological 'therapy' for these patients, but as the report and similar strong statements in the *British Medical Journal* have suggested, psychological interventions should be integral to good cancer care.

Medical 'blind spots'

A general hospital alleviates and cures many conditions. This is the reward most sought after by those in the vocations of nursing and medicine. The medical and nursing staff is for the most part young and they may have no experience of life in a household containing, for example, a very ill person or where someone has died. With conditions such as injuries and lacerations, infectious diseases and illnesses that are cured, it is possible for nurses and doctors to feel that they know what the patient feels. They might have had similar conditions in their own lifetime. However, with cancer and the complexities of its treatment what the patient endures is unimaginable to most people. Nurses and doctors see human beings undergo changes that are difficult to identify from their past experience. Fantasy may replace 'not knowing', and doctors and others may act out of the certainty that they know what their patient will experience. Their own dread of death may affect their treatment of patients, with the result that they load the patient with sedatives to reduce their awareness. The doctor, in identifying him- or herself with the patient, believes that he or she would want oblivion.

Unfortunately, many nurses and doctors, having seen many cancer patients, claim expertise in managing 'end of life' situations. What happens then is that there is a blanket prescription for all patients with cancer and the belief there is nothing more to learn. The cancer patient can easily become a stereotype in the eyes of those who care for them. A psychotherapeutic approach, by contrast, refuses to categorise patients in this way and the procedure involves adaptation to the individual rather than classification of the individual.

More training needed

There is, therefore, a need for greater and closer supervision of those working with cancer patients. The supervision of nurses and doctors, modelled on the training for psychotherapists and consisting of weekly meetings with an appropriately trained professional, such as a senior psychotherapist, would go a long way to establishing a supportive network. The senior psychotherapist could discuss the nurses' or doctors' interviews with their patients and some of the problems attached to dealing with serious illness. In talking to patients about their illness and its treatment, nothing should be interposed between the doctor and his or her subject. There should be no instruments and no medicine; the doctor in their person, instead, is the 'instrument' who conveys information, explores, interprets, and is the catalyst for the development of insight. Dealing with patients confronting death is a responsibility that requires skill and sensitivity, and these two qualities are often singularly undeveloped by medical training.

The formal training of medics does not prepare a doctor or a nurse for a psychotherapeutic role in treating patients, as there are no extended discussions about the feelings of individuals in pain. Young doctors are placed in a difficult position. They meet patients old enough to be their parents or grandparents with distressing difficulties and problems for which there appears to be no consolation or advice, and they may feel at a terrible loss, for there is no way of simulating 'walking in the shadow of death'.[3] No one really and properly know what it feels like to be in pain and physical decline.

As a doctor, I was made aware of this deficiency. I approached the patient with the aim of acquiring information by examination and questioning, so that I could identify the disease and place the patient in an illness category that I knew of from experience and training. I could then prescribe treatment appropriate for the condition and predict the course it would take considering generalisations about the disease's process. A psychiatrist may use the physical model of disease and consider mental 'disturbance' as if it were a physical illness. The patient is a 'case', and has the common features of that psychiatric illness. However, it is my opinion that this psychiatric approach has little to offer the patient with a serious physical illness. The distress and the depression are not the symptoms of a 'mental' illness. In fact, severe depression – familiar to me in psychiatric hospitals – never occurred in any of the hospitals I worked in.

As a psychoanalytic psychotherapist, I considered the individual patient and divested myself of any preconceptions about this person, from whom I had to hear in order to know how they really felt about their life and condition. I could not prejudge the patient's feelings about the havoc cancer had wreaked in their lives. How could I? Each was unique and I did not know them or their resources, their family and social milieu. I might be appalled by the physical damage, but I never really knew how far psychotherapy dealt with it. Experience also taught me that the most unexpected, sometimes original reactions, could occur and surprise me, so I never closed my mind to the unexpected.

In general medicine, detecting new and abnormal growths of tissue is also, as every medical student is taught, of salient importance. To 'miss' a cancer is a diagnostic sin. The emphasis is on diagnosis; the illness is explained by deduction and the discovery is a triumph. We think of the body as having systems for processing materials that enter it and cancer damages by blocking a healthy function, process or system in the body. The general perception of cancer, however, is that cancer does not interfere with functions but invades, like a parasite, corrupting and poisoning the system. This is due to the power and influence of cancer expressed in terms of a military metaphor (cancer as the enemy) in modern Western culture.

Entering the patient's 'inner world'

The psychotherapeutic approach, in contrast, sees a patient as a unique personality and it does not attempt to classify. The patient has an idiosyncratic view of the world and by listening, the therapist is given an entrée to this world view. The patient's 'inner world'[4] and what they do in it determines how they act in the 'real' world, the designated 'outside world'. Access to that inner world enables the psychotherapist to understand why a person thinks and acts as they do, rather than guess and generalise about what 'people' feel. The 'patient', from the psychotherapeutic viewpoint, is not a container of disease or a machine with a fault challenging one's skill at finding out what is wrong. Rather, the patient is in a unique situation, which the advent of cancer has changed dramatically. The significance of life issues, such as personal relationships and work that were previously considered by the patient to be all-important, may well become after the diagnosis 'a waste of time'. The psychotherapeutic process should be attentive to both dramatic and subtle shifts in perspective.

So, what are the key features of psychotherapy with cancer patients, and how is its deployment in a busy hospital setting different from that of a more traditional private practice? To what extent can the regularity and peculiarity of psychoanalytic psychotherapy be transferred to a more public space where time and confidentiality are thought to be difficult to manage and protect? And what valuable insights and effects does this particular form of therapeutic treatment offer to the patient suffering from cancer?

Taking time

The usual exchanges between doctors or nurses and patients are overshadowed by the constant possibility of interruption, and this seriously affects the quality of communication. The discourse between health professionals and patients has to be hurried and there is an inherent inequality in this relationship. The doctor can leave (and is often always on the verge of leaving) and the patient, being in bed or too weak to move, is left waiting. The 'history-taking' by the doctor is predetermined to a large extent because the doctor, to make a diagnosis, suggests what may be wrong. The patient often confirms what is already suspected by the time he or she arrives in hospital. The avoidance of subjective feelings about the illness is the aim of most conversations in hospital. Banalities are exchanged and a cordiality is achieved, but no one has the time or resources to sit and listen to how patients feel about being ill with cancer. With someone ill with cancer, this kind of intercourse is vital.

When the psychotherapist says to the patient, 'We have an hour', he or she is transforming the usual hospital experience, because the unspoken message is, 'Whoever you are, howsoever we proceed, I give you this time because your life is precious. I have no preconceptions about you and I have no idea what will transpire as you speak.' The medical staff cannot isolate time in this way. Instead, their main objective is to look for patterns of illness and find the most economical and efficient ways of behaving and speaking to the very ill person, for whom life may be shortly ending.

In spite of a greater embrace of psychotherapy, it is still a rare experience for a patient to find that they are listened to whatever they say. In neurology there is still a tendency to 'demonstrate' in the tiered lecture theatres and this is especially so with cancer, for which there are so few remedies and cures. In the arena of clinical medicine, the 'history-taking' is concerned with the patients' answers to questions directed towards eliciting the pattern of symptoms that assigns them to a disease category. The time given to this is usually very limited and it is extended only in so far as it emphasises and illuminates the medical 'history'. But the freedom to say what they think or feel apart from the limiting format of questions, is not given. In hospital, patients describe how they have questions and feelings with regards to the consequences of their illness yet ward rounds and clinic consultations seem designed to prevent 'free' thinking or awkward questions. And there is invariably no privacy; on visits to the bedside and in the outpatient clinic the exchanges are often public.

Privacy and confidentiality

The provision of privacy and confidentiality is a key feature and it allows the patient to speak freely and intimately. In a general hospital, conversations of such privacy and intimacy are not expected by the patient, and the psychotherapist must indicate clearly that the conversation is not going to be relayed to any other person. The patient in hospital has a particular understanding of 'confidentiality' as it means, in effect, 'only to other doctors and nurses' and not to relatives or other patients. What the psychotherapist must guarantee is that confidentiality is total; only the patient and the therapist know what is said. If this is not achieved, then there are limits to what the patient is prepared to say. If confidentiality is not assured, then the patient tends to speak with caution and an awareness of what they say and how it might affect other people.

A basic requirement then is the therapist's ability to guarantee privacy and to be trusted to keep to the vow. At the outset, when I was working with cancer patients, I explained that I did not follow the usual hospital procedures, that I would not put anything in the clinical notes other than a note to record the date of our meeting and when another is to take place. This ensured that staff knew when I was visiting the patient and when the patient was to be made available – without interruption – to be seen by me. I specified that I would not transmit the content of our exchanges to any other doctor, including their general practitioner, except in general terms at the patient's request. Similarly, I would not transmit any information to their relatives. I would also remind the patient that many relatives and doctors alike may be disconcerted by this embargo and that such confidentiality may produce difficulties. Doctors may feel that they are the confidants of their patients and they may become angry that a psychotherapist takes them over and does not follow the usual rules whereby doctors tell each other anything about their patients. Relatives may also feel excluded, but the very ill patient has often to be protected from relatives, who can infantilise the sick person. It is as if the sick patient is deemed to have lost their capacity for independent thinking and needs an advocate. The approach of psychotherapy, which treats the patient as an individual with the power to make decisions affecting his life and affording him the opportunity to express himself secretly, in effect, can become very unpopular with some relatives and medical staff.

Constancy

The psychoanalytic technique involves keeping the conditions for sessions as constant as possible. In ordinary circumstances this is to facilitate the process of uncovering the deeper meanings between verbal exchanges and descriptions. The patient experiences what is in their mind and if the environment is constant then inner changes are less likely to be attributed to external factors. To this end the psychoanalyst has the same room and the same furniture, adopts the same procedure each meeting, keeps meticulously to the appointed time and is above all careful to protect the sessions from interruptions. In a hospital this has to be modified. Constant surroundings are not possible and patients have to be seen wherever possible, on the ward or in the outpatients department. In a hospital there is no time to waste. The conditions change, as patient and psychotherapist speak, and from time to time. People pass close by on the wards and patients lie in the next bed. The same patient might be seen in different places, in different rooms or on the ward. The only constant is the psychotherapist, keeping to his or her promise to stay with the person whatever their state of mind amidst the hustle and bustle of the hospital.

Keeping appointments

Keeping a promise to come and see a bedridden person at a certain time indicates respect for them and their time. It means that the psychotherapist is taking care of them and their association, and is keeping them 'in mind' in order to return as arranged. It also indicates that they are in an egalitarian relationship, that their time is no less important than the psychotherapist's, and that the psychotherapist has time for them regardless of their physical and mental state.

Internal arrangements for patients in hospital are generally chaotic with regards to time. Appointments made in the outpatients department are not kept or patients are told to attend a clinic but not informed when they will be seen. Patients in hospital do not have visits and investigations at set times. If a time is given, it is rarely adhered to and no one expects it to be binding. It is important for the psychotherapist, I found, *to make appointments and keep them.* This was particularly important with patients in bed in hospital. It was in striking contrast to the rest of their experience and was evidence of a different approach. Languishing for long periods with nothing to do or waiting their turn to go down for an investigation makes the promised, timely visit an important occasion. The significance of these arrangements is different for patients who do not have cancer. But time for the cancer patient is particularly precious. It is often perceived as quickly 'running out'. To have someone to whom they can speak to privately and intimately is unique in their experience.

Meeting for the first time

Meeting a patient for the first time required me to give some indication as to why I was there and how we would proceed. I would say, depending on the circumstances, that I had been asked by their doctors or nurses to see them. I might say what the reason appeared to be from the referral note or letter, or simply that it was thought that I might be able to help. I was the only one of the medical staff not to wear a white coat. I said that I was a psychiatrist and a psychoanalytic psychotherapist and assured them that it was in the latter capacity as someone dealing with someone's thoughts and feelings that I was seeing them and not because they were considered to be mentally ill.

I allocated a period of time to our discussion. If it was possible I would spend approximately one hour with each patient. I would say at the outset how much time was going to be taken or approximately the actual time when we would finish. This was very important in a hospital setting where patients were never given this amount of time for freedom of speech. It indicated that it was not going to be the usual exchange – brief, often brisk conversation, terminated by the other party. A patient who does not know how much time they have to talk is limited in what they think they may broach.

In introducing myself I would say that I did not know how I could be of help. If they would try to say whatever they thought and felt, then we would see what would eventuate. Often my introduction was very brief and I would ask what was happening from their point of view. We were not embarking upon a discussion of the physical treatment but on how life was at that time for them.

Depending on the individual circumstances I would vary my procedure and with someone very ill I would arrange to return the next day or in two days. With others I would say that I would see them weekly. Some were seen only once.

The patients that I saw were invariably without any knowledge of psychoanalysis or theories of the unconscious mind. This did not matter. I was applying the principles of psychoanalysis to the psychotherapeutic exchanges between us, which means, for example, that I was interested in whatever that came into their mind, whatever they said and however they expressed themselves. I was interested in their dreams and in what the subtexts were beneath their narrative of events. Unlike in private psychoanalytic practice, I charged no fee and there was no deafening silence from me. I responded to what the patient said. I did not respond by saying nothing. There was a contract, but not a business one, for I contracted to be as available as possible. The patient, however, was under no obligation to accept. This approach varied only in detail according to the patient's physical condition. There were patients who were deaf and patients who could not communicate by speech, but exchanges were still possible by other means.

The therapeutic relationship

The relationship between myself and the majority of cancer patients developed quickly and intensely. I was constant, apart from the external hospital conditions described above, in that my arrival was predictable and I was imperturbable. I was neither frightened nor confident. I was not pitying or dismissive. I was accepted as a person who could accept them and their fears. It was reminiscent for some of them of a very early relationship with another – often a parent – that could contain them and their weal. I was frequently taken in – introjected – by the patient as a processor of bad feelings. By my demeanour and behaviour I did not contradict their expectations of me. I showed my belief in their potential and worth, and often their dread would give way to hopefulness.

A process came into being with the meeting. The exchanges did not stop when I left the patient. On many occasions, patients described how our discussions continued in their mind between sessions or after a session. I say 'after a session' because sometimes a second meeting was brief with an acknowledgement of what had transpired in the patient's mind. An illustration of this occurred when I came to see a man for the second time. I thought he was unconscious and judging by his breathing I thought that he was dying and that he would not regain consciousness. To my surprise he opened his eyes and roused himself to tell me that what I had told him at our previous one and only meeting had helped him! He had me in mind and wanted to leave me with a good feeling, to allay any fears I might have that I was useless. He was looking after me!

Protecting the patient

The psychotherapeutic process often had to be protected. I was open-minded about a patient when that person had already been classified as 'putting it on'. When this happened, the patient, for example, was thought to have 'imaginary' symptoms or worse, to be exaggerating. If a doctor asked me to see a patient considered to be 'hypochondriacal', generally the nurses had made the same diagnosis. I was in their opinion giving the patient too much undeserved attention. I was then the object of their disapproval.

Hostility, when it occurs towards a patient, is dangerous and is never justified. It is dangerous in that it blinds staff to the reality, which may involve real distress. In some cases, the signs of distress are not visible and the patient must then be treated psychologically as well as physically. Such a negative reaction is an illustration of the effects of the process in the 'inner worlds' of healthy carers. It is a process whereby they see exaggeration and duplicity in others, and the force of the conviction indicates the force with which they *must* see 'acting out', 'attention seeking', 'showing off' to the doctor. The result may be prejudice against the patient and an arrogance in observers, be they doctors or nurses. Occasionally, this confrontational attitude obscures the reality that the patient has cancer and is very ill.

Prejudice against the patient

Nurses and doctors may set aside their own experience and irrationally allege that the patient's symptoms are not 'genuine'. Most people in hospital, for example, know about fainting, and how it can be due to something in the mind. Furthermore, they know that the thoughts and feelings that produce the faint and the faint itself are not under conscious control. Often the person who faints would dearly like to do something to avoid it happening, particularly if they are a student nurse or doctor. But rational refutation has no effect. As the poet, Ogden Nash, puts it, the door of the bigot's mind opens outwards, and the harder one pushes against it the more tightly shut it becomes.[5] The prejudice against the patient can take many forms. It could be a belief that the patient could return to work. It could be a religious prejudice. On one cancer ward, the Sister in charge believed that the irreligious would not suffer so much if they had religion. A common form of prejudice manifested itself in believing the opposite of what the patient said. A patient who strenuously expresses a wish to go home but requires some help to do so is accused of not really wanting to go home and the complaint that the patient wants help is regarded as indicating that they really want to stay in hospital. Sometimes the patient is said to have given up and they may die as a result.

Full awareness

A man who had been on a boat that had suddenly turned over remembered, so he thought, the sequence of events. It was some time later before he realised that he had an unconscious memory. He recalled where he stood alongside a partition and as the boat turned over the partition became horizontal with his friends underneath and himself on top. Some weeks later, when he heard the sound of smashing crockery fallen from a table, he suddenly became unconscious and fell to the ground. This was the sound he heard when the boat began to turn over, because the tables had just been laid for dinner. The man lost consciousness repeatedly if without warning he heard the sound of breaking glass or crockery.

This is an unconscious process similar to the phenomenon where someone faints at the sight of blood or on hearing some very bad news. It is a process that is psychological but with profound physiological consequences. In a faint one becomes dead to the world. Consciousness is switched off. The import of what is happening cannot be assimilated and the emotion is overwhelming.

There are internal situations that can send the person into a deep sleep, ending with death. In contrast, there may be an awakening to a reality which can be acted on rather than reacted to. In the half-dreaming state, it is the unpleasant, hurtful things that surface. In the half-awake state, the delicate, beautiful, creative powers are lost. The mental debris repeatedly emerges whereas in full awareness new ways of seeing are found. When patients have anaesthetics that produce incomplete unconsciousness, it is the repugnant, violent and unpleasant thoughts and feelings that come to the surface because the defences that can, only in full consciousness, be mobilised, are rendered useless and weak. This is an important issue with serious illnesses because the most commonly used drugs reduce consciousness. With a serious illness full consciousness may be needed to be able to choose which way to go rather than to drift away. 'Full awareness' is not always encouraged, however, and the person with full awareness of their condition can be disconcerting to the doctors and nurses.

Dreams

Dreams are important features of thinking and patients in psychotherapy intuitively realise their significance and normally tell them spontaneously. Patients who are very ill may not mention them but they are invariably serious when they are mentioned as being of interest and possible importance. In psychotherapy, the significance of dreams may not immediately be apparent, but with cancer patients, the patient often realised their significance and the procedure was abbreviated. I often felt that I could propose an explanation or tentatively describe what I thought the dream portrayed. This would lead to a discussion of my interpretation, which often helped the patient to understand the salient problem. They would think about features of their life directed by the dream and discuss its relevance to the present.

Big car dream

A youth aged 15 was referred urgently by his physician, a young doctor. The anxiety of the doctor was considerable. He feared the patient's reaction because he felt that if he was himself the patient and learned that he was beyond hope and was going to die, then he would be inconsolable and terrified to the point of madness. The doctor had no idea of how to control, relieve or remove the anxiety of the patient.

The patient and I spent an hour together at the first meeting. The length of time and the content of our discussion intrigued the patient. When he was offered further sessions he accepted readily.

On one occasion he volunteered a dream. He was driving along a dual carriageway in a very large car. Despite the car being very large it did not have very much power. I said the dream might represent his fear that though he was a big man (he was above average in height and build), he felt persecuted by the disease and felt that he was going to be overwhelmed and become weak and powerless. He responded by saying, 'You meant that I react like this to the doctors?' He went red and said, 'It's funny that you should say that because two or three weeks ago that was just what I was thinking about myself.'

He then started a discussion of dreams by commenting that they 'really do mean something!' He said it was a shock to realise that there is a part of the mind over which you have no control and which you are not conscious of. He asked how it could be influenced and we discussed how it could not be controlled or accessed directly, but indirectly via dreams and associations. My rough interpretation of his dream had changed his view of dreams and his feelings about himself. He said that he was stopped in his tracks by what I had suggested and this he said was very unusual, because he was never usually 'lost for words'.

The diagnosis of cancer can terminate an individual's enjoyment of the present. He cannot plan for the future or live in the present, even if there is no pain or disfigurement. The cancer is perceived to permeate everything. In the following case, a young man, through psychotherapy, reverses this and learns to enjoy life on his own terms.

Living for the present

The patient was a 20-year-old student who had a recurrence of meningioma. He had his first operation in his own country when he was a medical student.

After the operation he had to drop out of the course. He had a further operation and the tumour was thought to be more malignant than was at first thought and further treatment with radiotherapy was proposed. The nurses thought he was depressed and needed to be transferred to a psychiatric unit. Without speaking to him they assumed that he was suicidal. They had taken special precautions and had locked the windows in his room to which he was confined. I was asked to arrange his transfer to a psychiatric hospital.

He seemed so depressed and timorous when I first met him that I saw him each day for the next four days. At first it seemed that he was depressed simply because he was ill and this had taken him away from his normally very active life at university. He had been prescribed antidepressant drugs and I immediately began reducing the daily dosage. I intended stopping them altogether. When I saw him on the fourth day he appeared less depressed. He was more lively and alert as the drugs had been markedly reduced. What worried him now was a change in his potency. This upset him and was in line with his distressing feeling of being generally inadequate. His parents had visited him between our sessions and he had told them to leave. He said that he could not stand the anxieties that they generated.

I arranged for him to be discharged and to begin seeing me for sessions outside the hospital. He had two older brothers, both successful dentists practising in this country, and one of them lived in London. He could live with him.

He was worried about his memory and he was afraid that he might lose his temper with his parents as they tended to treat him like a little boy. His consultant had secured for him a provisional place at a London teaching hospital to study dentistry. He had three months to decide if he wanted to commence his course. His first visit to London had been precipitated by an epileptic fit followed by a drinking bout. There were two more fits.

An encephalogram had been mildly abnormal and antiepileptic drugs were prescribed. Subsequently a large cyst in his brain was found to be present. But the epileptic fits and the need for two operations on his brain profoundly disturbed him and he felt very insecure. He had been very competitive in sport and in education and now he felt that he had been rendered ineffectual.

He came to my private consulting room as an outpatient regularly several times a week.

When I first met him I introduced myself and said that he should come to see me if there was any way in which I could help, if he felt that he would like to try and tell me whatever was in his mind. I was completely open-minded about him. I was not influenced by what I had been told by the nursing staff, who did not know him either. I sensed that they were frightened of him, and they perceived him as a depressed, suicidal young man. Many of the nurses were his contemporaries and many of the doctors could envisage the disappointment that they would have felt if the same thing had happened to them. They were identifying features in the patient, however, that did not exist.

I did not ask questions that would have indicated what I thought was important. I had no preconceptions and I made myself available with an introduction encouraging him to say whatever he wished. He never mentioned the nurses' thoughts about him and appeared to be unaware of their feelings about him. The first thing he spoke about was a recent weekend when he had gone with two prostitutes and found that he could not ejaculate. This depressed him. It was a disconcerting change, unexpected in his body. He had not spoken to any one about this. It was a side effect of the drugs he was taking, which included antidepressants. He said that while he was in therapy his friends would be now well advanced on their medical course and he would be unable to catch them up. He felt that after the second operation he would no longer be able to play squash as he had done for the first team of his university. He never mentioned suicide and the general tenor of the discussion was his feeling that in all respects he was now rendered impotent. Most strikingly, with the reduction and cessation of his medication for depression he became more alert and lively.

The salient points of his psychotherapy were the ways in which he regarded the brain tumour. He felt ashamed of it, as if he was responsible. He felt inferior as if it was something avoidable. He went out with a girl who asked him what he had been doing in London for the past six months. He said that he had been ashamed to tell her and said that he was looking for work having given up dentistry. He said that he had feelings of inferiority when he first took girls out and the brain tumour had just made these feelings worse.

In the sessions he went over his life saying that he had had so many opportunities to be cultured and acquire knowledge and become skilled, but he knew nothing and had done nothing: 'it has all been wasted!' He spoke as if he had forgotten the brain tumour, the two operations and the anxieties of adolescence. He was a lonely young man, always vulnerable, it seemed, and now with his ambitions thwarted, he felt crushed and his fantasy of failure confirmed.

Life, he realised, had not changed when he had the brain tumour. It always contained possibilities, some known, some unknown. The illusion before the cancer was that everything could be predicted and controlled. Now the best he could do was to live and make arrangements in the present. He applied and was accepted for a dentistry course. He eventually stopped coming for sessions. He went on a ski-ing holiday with his siblings. An epileptic fit soon after, however, signalled the return of the brain tumour and within a few days he was in a coma and died in hospital.

In the sessions this young man was able to debate with himself old arguments. They provided him with an opportunity to discuss his life so far, and consider how he could live. He started driving again, to test himself out, and began more physical activities, culminating in the ski-ing holiday. He lived and planned for the present without referring to the brain tumour. No one knew if it would recur and he had no symptoms.

The inner debates of some patients can arrive at conclusions that can account for sudden changes of mood. Nursing staff may be confused, being unable to see any external reason for the change. In medicine and nursing the search is mostly for a single cause – the 'causative factor' – and, once found, further inquiry stops and there is a self-imposed blindness to other possibilities. There may be confusion and dismay when a single cause cannot be found. In the case of the following patient confusion arose because she had been very downcast for a variety of reasons.

The enemy within

The patient had been assured, after a mutilating operation for cancer of the vulva, that it would not return. When it did two years later she said she was 'shattered'. The medication she was given had to be stopped because it produced nausea and the radiotherapy produced burning and pain. After being admitted to hospital she appeared to be in good spirits and pain-free. The senior nurse on the ward was confused. She did not know if the patient knew her condition or even what was wrong with her. The nurse thought this because the patient initially seemed in such good spirits and, putting herself in the patient's place, she did not see how she could be relatively cheerful. The reason I was asked to see this woman was that the patient's mood changed and she seemed to the nursing staff to be very confused. They did not know whether she wanted to go home or stay in hospital.

This woman told me that she had been planning to go on holiday to Norway, and then after returning to work, fulfil a life-long ambition and go on safari. This explained to me the apparent good mood she was in when she first came into hospital. It was not due to the environment, but to an inner voice that said that she could still look forward to plans made before the diagnosis of cancer. She knew exactly her condition, but she debated internally the precarious condition she was in. Something could happen suddenly. The cancer had eroded the wall of a large artery and a sudden unstoppable haemorrhage could occur at any time. She lived in another part of the country and it would take several hours to get home. She was afraid to leave the hospital. She had a stepdaughter who was devoted to her and wanted her to come home so she could nurse her. The patient asked herself if she could let her do this.

The stepdaughter had just managed to get a job that she had wanted for some time. If her stepmother, the patient, went home, then she would have to give up her job. I said that it appeared to me that she knew the risk in going home that something might happen to her before she got there. The patient had steadfastly said that she would not have any more treatment. The stepdaughter, if she went home, would be given the opportunity to express her love and would feel that she had been effective and kind to her stepmother. I was agreeing with one view of the situation that she held. She could decide the way to proceed. She could take a chance and a risk in order to achieve something constructive. The only certainty in her situation was her resolve.

The process that came into being with our meeting was in the nature of a debate. The protagonists in her mind were the seductive, generating phantasies that all will be well (safari plans will happen); the 'play safe' counterargument to stay where she is and not move from hospital; and, against these voices, the heartfelt request from inside to look after those who love her and whom she felt would give up their life for her.

She decided that she wanted to go home, but she felt that this would compromise her stepdaughter as there was a risk that she might have a haemorrhage on the train. One of the nurses on the ward, however, who was affected by this woman's dilemma, volunteered to accompany her home on the train.

This woman did reach home safely, but she died two days after. All her family were present. Her husband wrote a letter to me expressing the family's joy at the shared two days together which he referred to as a 'wonderful time'.

There would seem to be an enemy within activated by the cancer situation, formulating negative ideas as in the instances described. The sufferer is told that their life is finished, over, and this reduces them to waiting, powerless, for death. The options as they appear to these patients, in the first instance, include passivity and the acceptance of negative, life-stopping ideas. They do not see how they might achieve an independence of the physical state. The psychotherapeutic process attempts to dissolve some of the phantasies in the inner world of the patient, and by making interpretations of the way the inner voices compete and counterargue, the therapist can clarify things. The interpretations are not instructions to the patient, or admonitions or reassurances. They do not aim to show what should be or what could be, but merely and simply what is. In the case of this patient, she was able, with her voices mapped out by the therapy, to take charge of her life and to act in a way that allowed people to care for her and which repaid their concern and love.

Projecting despair into others

There were patients whose internal world was so collapsed by the cancer that nothing could be taken in. They could not begin to express their feelings, and there appeared to be no room, no possibility even, for a container of their feelings. In two instances, both young married men, I was asked to see them because they had stopped talking. They did not respond to their wives, and from the accounts of events preceding the cancer I could only surmise that they had succumbed to destructive forces within. In each case there had been an unprepared-for failure of all treatment and no prospect of further treatment. The men felt that their life had ended. What appeared to produce despair was their projection of this view into others. No one in their minds could find them worth talking to or working with, and so they stopped talking. Physically they did not have pain or feel unwell. They were conscious and able to speak, but felt browbeaten by inner voices which said that no one could be bothered to listen.

To live while alive

I was asked to see a married couple urgently. The patient was a young woman with an inoperable cancer of the breast for which there was no further active treatment. The husband kept breaking down and crying. The woman herself had stopped talking to him and she was, out of character, not responding to news he brought of the children.

I saw the distraught husband. No help had been forthcoming from anyone and he was bewildered and desperate. His wife, he said, had been a competent, strong woman and of them both, was the stronger. He could not cope with the prospect of being without her, and having been told that she was going to die and that there was no further treatment, he felt he could not cope with her care.

It seemed to me as if he was treating his wife as if she was already dead. For him her life was already over and his behaviour, the weeping and desolation, indicated to her that there was no point in talking. There was no point in talking to her because she had no future. I suggested that his view was a death sentence upon his wife and that she must feel therefore that there was no point in talking to him. My intervention was to demonstrate this impasse between the couple and to suggest that once the death sentence was lifted, there was much that was worthwhile in life in the present. She then began to talk again. The rationale in both their minds was what is the point in talking to someone if they are going to die, particularly if one doesn't know exactly when? For the majority of people this is the case, I pointed out, whether they have cancer or not, and this view severely restricts the vitality and love in a relationship.

I acted as a catalyst in this case, facilitating communication between two people who loved one another but who had succumbed to a view that held that life was already over – which it most certainly was not.

In this chapter, I have attempted to give some sense of the way that cancer in its many forms affects the mind of the sufferer and the carer in a negative way with anxiety, dread, despair and hopelessness. The mind that is so affected can profoundly influence bodily processes, and extreme hopelessness produce death. In the internal world of the sufferer, persecutory feelings may grow up around the fantasy of cancer as a pervasive, intrusive, living parasite, and these feelings may be stimulated by the reactions of others, who also live in fear of the disease. In the following chapter, I take a closer look at the patient/doctor interaction in the hospital and the way in which it is often difficult within a medical context to retain a sense of self.

Notes

1   Calman–Hine Report, by the Expert Advisory Group on Cancer and the Chief Medical Officers of England and Wales, London: Department of Health, 1995.
2   *British Medical Journal*, 320 (2000), 59.
3   Ibid.
4   This is a term first used by Melanie Klein to describe an individual's thoughts, feelings and perceptions. These may bear no relation to experienced reality, but for the individual they constitute an inner reality by which external reality is experienced and judged.
5   Taken from Ogden Nash's poem, 'Seeing Eye to Eye is Believing'.

Chapter 3

The impact of cancer on hospital relationships

An individual who is diagnosed with cancer tends to lose his or her established sense of self in the community and in the hospital world becomes a cipher. This kind of marginalisation makes patients extremely vulnerable and their relationships, both internal and external to the hospital environment, can be seriously undermined as a consequence. This chapter considers the hospital world and the complex of relationships within it. The presence of a professional figure able to negotiate the dread and fear of both patients and the medical staff is vital to the treatment and cure of cancer.

Entering hospital

In the main entrance of the Royal Marsden Hospital, a large notice board covered in announcements of meetings about cancer in various anatomical regions greeted all visitors. The notices were a distinctive feature of this hospital. They advertised what it did and how doctors spent their time. There were many meetings occurring regularly every week; there was specialisation with separate groups for different parts of the body or different forms of cancer and 'casualty' rates – in other words, statistics were a preoccupation. The bold headings on notices advertised: 'Head and Neck review meeting'; 'Testicular Cancer'; 'Breast unit breakfast meetings'; 'Solid Tumour Group'. There were no messages for patients – or for nurses for that matter. Turning away from these messages for the high command – the 'generals' of hospital medicine – the newcomer was brought down to earth and to his or her place by the cheerful enquiry from the porter's window. Porters directed new patients by their bodily parts. 'Breast Clinic'; 'Radiotherapy – head? Dr Blond – brain tumour'; 'Head and Neck ward'.

This kind of depersonalisation, a defence against painful reality, is found most strikingly in the army where individuals become 'casualties' and 'personnel' 'proceed', go to 'ablutions' and are 'discharged'. The aim of both military and medical professionals is to deny the reality of the suffering and the losses; and remain 'uninvolved'. The person ceases to exist and instead there is the 'patient', a cipher for the person unnoticed. The quiet, uncomplaining patient is a marginalised person in the hospital world. Patients who do protest are avoided – generally they are feared for being 'bolshy' and awkward. In some cases the protesting patient is deliberately neglected.

On entering the cancer hospital, patients leave the familiar in their daily life for another world, where the unimaginable holds sway and they are powerless to alter anything. Few ask questions and even fewer protest or leave. The majority are passive participants, afraid to offend or stand out. Exposed to conditions unprecedented in their individual lives, it is as if like soldiers they are going to war. Patients told for the first time that they are suffering from cancer appear stunned, mute and dazed, as if they have shell shock. Doctors and nurses, brisk and alert, walk between and around the wounded and the dying. There are few exchanges between the patients and doctors, who wear expressions on their faces that give nothing away and who pass among the condemned. Statistics are everything. The battle against cancer is a manoeuvre against the enemy and, as in war, there is a scrupulous avoidance of reality. Staff on the cancer ward are trained to avoid the whole truth about an individual's condition and, like the recruiting sergeants, they lie. They avoid long conversations with the suffering, conversations that may lead to intimacy, awkward questions and the truth.

The 'other' place

In every community there are certain places seen out of the corner of the mind's eye, places where 'other' people go – cemeteries, crematoria, mental hospitals, cancer hospitals. Patients arriving at a cancer hospital have to confront themselves in a new way; they become the 'other', the kind of person who is marginalised through having a potentially life-threatening disease. These patients arrive in a devastated state, having had 'the news', the results of a test, a routine examination, conveyed with the heart-sinking phrases that everyone knows: 'I'm sorry to have to tell you . . .'; 'Unfortunately it doesn't look too good'; 'They've found a "tumour"/ "growth"/"obstruction" that needs looking into . . .'. However phrased, it all signifies 'cancer'. Inside the hospital, every attempt is made to avoid using the word 'cancer' to patients. There is a code that staff utilise to indicate that cancer is present. Terms such as 'neoplasm' (new growth of cancer), 'mitotic disease' (an allusion to the splitting of chromosomes when cells multiply), 'space-occupying lesion' (usually reserved for brain tumours) are common, and as these terms become familiar to patients so they are discreetly changed for others. This meta-language signals to both patients and staff that something too much to bear has happened.

Consultants who use these code terms at the first meeting with a sick patient are often attempting to put themselves in the patient's place, which, from the consultant's point of view, appears full of dread and unbearable despair. It is difficult for the healthy professional to imagine that the patient might be feeling anything else. This dread and despair may actually be the consultant's but they are feelings in the consultant's mind that are shifted on to the patient. This has two important consequences. The consultant thinks he or she knows how the patient feels, even though the patient's state of mind remains unexplored and un-met, and the patient is immediately alerted via this projection to the seriousness of the situation. Why the secrecy, the patient may wonder? If the experts are behaving in this way, then what is the fate that awaits me? It can only be death.

Military metaphors are commonplace in the cancer hospital. We are all familiar with them. Cancer can be 'aggressive' or 'non-aggressive', 'invasive' or 'non-invasive'. Cancer is defined in terms that suggest the Enemy. It is singular in generating awe and apprehension in the minds of both sufferer and 'carer'. There are other diseases with unpleasant consequences but their names are not kept from lay people in the same way. The fantasy of cancer as an alien parasitic invader creates a special kind of fear, as Susan Sontag in her book, *Illness as Metaphor* (1978), has described, and this fear is greater or lesser depending on which part of the body is inhabited and attacked by the cancer 'parasite'.[1] As I show in the next chapter, cancer arising in the mouth, for example, is perceived to be more repellent and devastating than cancer arising further away from the head, in, for example, the bowel, because the central location of the self is perceived to be in the mouth. As one moves away from this locus, the sense of self becomes increasingly remote and some detachment is possible.

The hospital world

The patient's journey begins with the referral to a hospital or diagnostic centre for cancer. These are stations representing the move away from normal life to another life of hospital visits, investigations and treatment. The hospital world is an unfamiliar world and when a patient enters he or she feels immediately different from those who work in it; for the patient this world inspires awe and trepidation, for the staff it is unthreatening and familiar. In the mind of the patient, hospital life is bipartite: there are those with cancer and those without, 'others' who look on. Now the patient is part of the cancer treatment world he or she is a passive traveller on a journey that others determine. At this point, the patient needs special sympathetic care. The patient needs *parri passu* with the medical investigations, to be enveloped in the arms of the hospital with staff willing and able to take the emotional load. This requires an approach that considers the person not just the disease, but doctors and nurses tend to be always doing something practical or technical. As a result, the patient is left feeling on the sidelines. In the past, outpatient departments used to be managed by a senior nurse who ensured that patients were cared for and no one was abandoned to cry alone. Today, particularly in the under-resourced and overstretched NHS hospitals in Britain, there is precious little time for staff to give emotional care to distressed patients. Priorities have changed in the NHS, and so has the concept of nursing. The idea of a motherly and wise corpus of nurses presiding over a ward of sick patients has been replaced by a fast turnover of physically and emotionally overstretched nursing staff, who have no time or training to deal with the demands of life and death situations.

The holistic treatment of cancer patients presents an enormous and complex dilemma for doctors and nurses overwhelmed by the pressures of hospital work. Not only are resources lacking but it is difficult for staff to know what to say or do that would make the patient's situation easier to bear. With regard to treating cancer patients in particular, hospital staff have to deal in their own minds with the 'unthinkable' – gross disfigurement, the loss of faculties (such as speech), isolation and death.

Inappropriate behaviour

Many patients appreciate the traumatic nature of their illnesses for those charged with their care, and they very often help by being kindly and unquestioning to set at ease those who look after them. This was brought home to me when I was sitting in an armchair at the centre of a ward.

There was a lot of traffic passing between the beds, and I was talking to a woman who had been referred to me. She was in her sixties and had originally come to Britain as a refugee from Germany. We were discussing Solzhenitsyn's book *Cancer Ward*.[2] As we sat there a young doctor who was passing noticed us. She came over, cut across our conversation, chucked the patient under her chin and declared 'You're smiling now!' and walked on. The patient said 'Yes' and nodded. She turned to me and shrugged her shoulders.

The young doctor had behaved towards this intelligent patient as if she were encouraging a child. In many ways the scenario was inevitable and understandable. The doctor was a gauche woman in her twenties trying to cope with being on the hospital stage. Socially inexperienced, but well meaning, she was conscious of her powerful professional role. Patients, in spite of their maturity, were looking to her to make decisions that would profoundly affect their lives. Not only had she the medical knowledge but she also had the power to initiate conversation with strangers of her parents' or grandparents' age. This was a new experience for them as well as for her, but as my patient demonstrated, patients invariably tolerated patronising behaviour by junior doctors. Cancer makes passive and grateful the most independent-minded of patients.

Cancer patients do not have to behave or think in this way. They can remain in a non-patient mode and demand recognition of their terrible plight. They can, like people trapped on a collapsing bridge, shout for help, but instead they tend to behave as though they are not worthy of assistance. They are for the most part docile, and unconsciously they may project into the hospital and its staff an inability to confront the truth about their illness. This can result in an unwitting collusion between patients and staff about being beyond help, for staff often share the fear of cancer and this can have a devastating effect on the psychological well-being of the patient. Staff have different ways of dealing with the painful issues of cancer and cancer death. One is to be in denial, reassuring themselves that it could never happen to them. This has the unfortunate consequence that they then may feel distant and different from the patients. Another strategy of defence is to focus on the physical pain, but not the mental pain or suffering. Their focus is often on the effects of the palliative treatment, reasoning that it is the best that they can do. Neither of these very understandable human defences involves thinking about the patient's feelings, and the patient as a result can feel very isolated. In this situation, the patient's distress needs to be met through the expression of sympathy and containment. Cancer patients in particular need to know that they are not alone, that the doctors and nurses will be present and involved to the end – whether the end be cure, remission or death. Sadly, patients who are dying are not given priority and no one special is allocated to these individuals.

Medical vulnerability

In the cancer hospital a bizarre situation influences the way that doctors and nurses think about themselves and their patients. They are before the patients as 'characters' walking on a stage. Patients and doctors are strangers to each other, thrown together in an arena, on the one side of which are the frightened and suffering, with embarrassment about 'undressing', meeting strangers, wondering what impression they will make, and what sort of person they will be allocated. On the other side, the doctors and nurses act nonchalantly, as if accustomed to the awe and deference they inspire. They can talk to anybody in any way they like. They can be flat and unemotional or patronising and polite or hearty and familiar. The doctors feel that they have to live up to expectations, with solutions at the ready and cheerful comments to assuage patients' feelings of doom. The young and inexperienced find themselves pushed into the assigned doctor role with strangers of all ages who they know have no power to choose whom they would like to see. This arrogance on the part of the medical staff is primitive. It is reminiscent of the child born rich and beautiful, the child born into royalty, who comes to believe that he is really important and a superior person. In the medical context, this kind of arrogance does not help develop a genuine sympathy for the sick. Instead the doctor, with his or her power, stands apart from the patients, who treat him or her with awe and obsequiousness.

Doctors may respond to patients' expectations, as they imagine them, by feeling a failure if they do not come up with some solution or a reassuring proposal. Nurses, too, feel that they should be able to make patients better, and patients do indeed make them feel better when they respond appropriately. But when patients do not say that they feel better, unwittingly they deprive the doctor or nurse of their enhanced status and they can feel very angry. Such patients may then become labelled as unappreciative, difficult, strange, or even as having a low pain threshold.

The vulnerability of patients and medical staff in the face of the dynamic I have described above is perhaps one of the most powerful arguments for the appointment of a psychotherapist, who is a professional with psychological expertise, but who is without the deific aura that surrounds physicians and surgeons. Within the hospital, there needs to be some recognition of the dynamic between the patient and the staff, and that in spite of the death sentence often conferred by cancer and the burden of patients' demands, staff too should feel more free to respond to patients' feelings. In the 'inner world' of the doctor or nurse, however, there is invariably a critical chorus that jeers unless they can solve problems and make patients feel better, but they should realise that they do not have to come up with cures and solutions for every aspect of cancer. They are not superhuman. The problem is that doctors and nurses are not trained to help with patients' emotional issues and they may feel criticised for this. This criticism can come from the inner chorus, but it may also be a product of external forces. The 'projections' of patients can make doctors feel very powerful, but these projections can be undermining of good treatment in that it inhibits the rapport between a patient and a doctor. They can act as smokescreens to the truth of the situation. The inherent arrogance of the world of medicine, borne of the power ascribed to those who determine life and death issues for sick and often frightened people, can be crippling to its professionals.

The 'bad' patient

At one of the hospitals I worked in, the nursing staff on one ward all registered their annoyance with one particular patient. Their complaints were that this woman never said that she felt better, whatever the nurses did for her. There was no expression of gratitude and she never said 'thank you'. In the minds of the nurses she was a 'bad object', and they gathered to this perception and fantasy all kinds of what appeared to be supporting evidence. For example, though she certainly had cancer there was doubt expressed in the medical notes as to what was actually causing her symptoms. The nurses interpreted this as meaning that her symptoms were not 'real', leading them to conclude that she was exaggerating her condition. This justified them in their anger towards her. In their view, she was undeserving of their concern and best nursing care.

In actual fact, the patient was very ill and had great difficulty in breathing, a problem compounded by terrific anxiety. She felt she was not going to recover and was worried about the lack of arrangements in place to take care of her 12-year-old child. She was a single parent with no relatives and no resources. The illness was fast becoming unbearable and she had not prepared for death. Nor had anyone else. No one attended to her dilemma. In medical terms, there was nothing that could be done to relieve the physical symptoms of her cancer. No one wanted to say 'You are going to die', and no attempt was made for care for the child or to alert an agency to do so. The nurses' defence against their realisation of this woman's dilemma and against a sense of their own impotence was to brand her a malingerer. The patient they held in their minds was of their own construction. She was a bad patient. Instead of loving attention in her hour of greatest need, she was abandoned, and she felt abandoned.

The 'good' patient

Many patients realise when a doctor or nurse does not know what to say or do. In many cases they sympathise with the doctor's inability to help and lie quietly as a consequence, without asking for help. The quiet uncomplaining patient may be suffering the most, but is regarded as the one giving the least trouble, a 'good' patient. This recalls the findings of research conducted by Bowlby and Robertson in the early 1950s, when they looked at the experience of children entering a hospital for children. In their study, they described a situation where children admitted to a children's ward were separated from their parents. At that time, parents were not encouraged to stay with their sick children or linger over the parting when they were admitted. This made the children 'worse', that is, distraught and crying. A brisk parting was the ideal and the Sister-in-charge took over instead. In this set-up, the child that did not cry and protest about being left – the quiet child – was deemed 'good' and thought to be less distressed than the child that screamed and cried. Bowlby and Robertson exploded the myth of the quiet-therefore-good patient, and they showed that the quiet child was frequently the most profoundly depressed.[3] Similarly, and by extension, it cannot be presumed that the uncomplaining, quiet and meekly grateful cancer patient is coping the best with the illness, its treatment and its effects and is not in great need of caring, continuous loving care.

First-name terms

After the first visit to hospital, or even at the first visit, the patient might be unaccompanied by relatives or friends. The patient sees the doctor, or the doctors and nurses in the team, and there is a charade of friendliness. The patient's first name may be used, and will be again in subsequent contacts. This is bizarre behaviour at one level, but it is intended to convey a friendly intimacy. Staff use first names to make themselves feel comfortable. The delusion is that they 'know' the patient, who feels welcomed and valued like the 'valued' client of hotel brochures. In some cases, however presumptuous and incongruous it may seem, first names may also be used by staff in referring to the patient's relatives. Proper names, however, can indicate 'respect' for the patient's importance and individuality.

A patient had been seeing the consultant regularly on her own for several years, with a form of cancer that was incurable and life-limiting. On one occasion, he saw that she was with her daughter and invited them both into the consulting room. Immediately using the daughter's first name and using the impersonal pronoun 'she' to refer to the patient, he gave a chilling and terrifying prognosis of how the illness would develop and how long 'she' would survive. The patient sat transfixed and appalled, as this was a different story to the one she had been told. There was a chill. The patient realised that for the consultant she did not exist as a person, and it felt to her as if the consultations had been a pretence in which he enjoyed himself at the expense of others. She also realised that he had forgotten that she was present and that he was, in effect, talking principally to her daughter. At one point the patient interjected to say 'I'm still here!' He seemed to her to be telling her daughter facts that she should not or would rather not hear.

In the doctor's mind, he had done no wrong, but in his eagerness to have a *tête-à-tête* with the daughter, he exposed his contempt for the patient and his callowness and insensitivity to both the mother and daughter. To cover up, he needed to be consistent about the way he delivered information. He exposed his real lack of feeling for the patient hidden beneath a veneer of first-name familiarity.

Lack of empathy

A surgeon was talking affably to his patient as he examined her in a room in the outpatient department. He knew her quite well. She was a professional writer and a sensitive and perceptive individual. To allow her to dress he drew the curtains round the couch and withdrew to the other side of the room. Only two metres away, he began speaking about her to another person in terms she did not recognise: the information was quite different from what he had told her when he saw her. Behind the curtain, she heard everything he had said, the details of which were confirmed later in his notes.

The lack of empathy in this surgeon's case, and in the case of the doctor above, signifies an inability on the professionals' part to understand how others might feel. This 'blindness' of the professionals to patients' emotional needs, whether they be sitting before them or hidden by ward curtains, can be very damaging to the traumatised patient's sense of self. Instead of thinking about how the patient might feel, professionals identify in the patient characteristics that are really projections of their own lack of feeling and comprehension. In both cases cited above, the patients were devastated and furious at their treatment, but they could do nothing about it.

Giving patients the opportunity to speak about anything they deem important is a rare and valuable freedom. Unfortunately, medical training and orientation can blind doctors and nurses to problems that patients have which are not about the disease but about their lives and relationships. These problems or concerns may be about 'life' in general: how, for example, to prepare others, their spouse or their children, for life after their death. Others have serious problems that they wish to see resolved before they die. Some have a burden of strong feelings that they wish to discharge by telling someone who understands their mental pain and suffering. The provision of privacy and confidentiality is important for these individuals and in some instances it is not fully realised how imprisoned a patient can feel in the hospital environment.

Personal space

Patients suffering from terminal illness require a clearly boundaried personal space because they can easily feel intruded on. One patient I encountered was not able to speak for himself. This was not due to his cancer, but his wife, who was always present and insisted that he was a 'quiet man' who could not speak for himself. She maintained that he was too modest and so she had to speak for him. His wife described how depressed he was and she wanted him 'medicated' for this. She gave an idealised account of his relationship with her and with his son, who kept urging upon him surgical procedures that had only a remote chance of being useful. Alone, however, the patient gave quite a different story; he wanted to be free to make his own decisions about treatment. He did not want another exploratory operation – his brother and father had had the same type of cancer and he 'knew the score'. He knew that it was now incurable despite the efforts of his wife and son to get a surgeon to look again.

The complex nature of the patient/doctor interaction rests mainly on the doctor's wishes to satisfy the patient's need to be seen by an all-knowing, decisive professional. In the doctor's mind, there may be a subtle identification with the patient, who looks up to doctors as confident specialists with no doubts in their mind about what they are doing. Because of this the doctor may feel that there is no need to be concerned about the patient. Both the patient and doctor need to trust the perception of the medical professional as all-knowing. Consequently, from this point of view, no inquiry is needed about that individual's state of mind. Moving among the wards of cancer patients doctors can wear a mantle of omniscience.

The value of psychotherapy

The cancer hospital, therefore, is a place where the staff are reacting to the effects that cancer has on both the patients and themselves. Fearful patients put their trust in whomsoever seems certain and positive, and this is usually the doctor or nurse treating them. But close identification with such a figure in the ways I have described above can be corrosive, because the truth about the patient's condition is not always clearly articulated and discussed. The aim of my intervention as a psychoanalytic psychotherapist was to reinstate the truth of the situation and provide an open and liberating space in which patients could articulate their thoughts. Exchanges between myself and the patients were in simple and direct language with no attempt on my part to reassure or avoid the truth about their physical condition.

I shared with the patient immediately what I knew from the referral note and from the case notes. This was in two parts – the physical state and its development and the reasons I was asked to see the patient. It might be explicit in the doctor's note, for example, that the patient 'complains of pain which cannot be relieved'; 'the outlook is poor and no further treatment is envisaged'; 'the patient is distressed', or other words might be used: 'complaining', 'demanding', 'afraid', 'poor domestic situation'. I would note what *appeared* to be the situation and then made it clear that I was not one of the doctors. I was sharing in a frank way my and their appraisal of this situation. Then I said I would stay and return to see them – whatever happened.

We might conclude that the cancer was now untreatable and the patient was going to die – sooner or later, but the patient almost invariably changed gear and was often relieved to know the situation. They would speak about their life and what was most important to them. The conversation moved away from the cancer and the physical state to features of their inner world. I listened and followed what they said, interpreting, clarifying where possible where I saw misconceptions, and sometimes I would interpose with alternative interpretations.

In my capacity as a psychoanalytic psychotherapist, I represented the opportunity of personal space, and I received my patients with a strong sense of duty and protective care. Soon after I began seeing patients in this way, it became apparent to me that my presence in the hospital was having a profound effect also on many of my medical and surgical colleagues. They felt supported by my interventions, and this led me to the conclusion that the principles that I evaluated and adhered to in my work with patients derived in part from my experience of psychoanalytic psychotherapy and offered a way of transforming the hospital care of patients coping with the demoralising effects of cancer.

Professional suspicion

During the hubbub of a staff Christmas party one doctor asked me what I said to a cancer patient of hers. 'That patient you spoke to . . . she really was better afterwards! What did you say?' It was clear that she had never expected 'just talking' to help her patient. She was more inclined to believe that there was a magic formula. If I told her what it was, she suggested, she could do the same thing. She did not think that any skill or training was involved. Another senior doctor said to me, whilst acknowledging the value of my work with his patients, that what I did could not be passed on to nursing staff. He said it was because it was too complicated for nurses, which was both a flattering and destructive comment to make to me. On the one hand, the work was diminished in value, and on the other, the mystique of what I did was being described as something that could not be 'passed on'. I suspected that behind both of these comments was fear and despair. The senior doctor favoured a cognitive rather than psychoanalytic-psychotherapeutic approach because it was easier to understand and therefore control. Cognitive therapy would not, in his view, affect his omniscience.[4]

When I started seeing cancer patients as a psychotherapist, my practice and procedures were under continual close scrutiny by the hospital staff. After about six months, I was gradually accepted as providing necessary support for both patients and staff. It did not take long for improvements to be registered and some senior doctors, who had originally opposed having a psychiatrist in the hospital, referred their relatives to me. There was therefore a change of considerable importance within the hospital system, effected without lectures, discussions or descriptions of method or principle. The most important consequence was that the status of patients rose – someone cared and staff wanted this both for themselves and for the ward/department in general. A burden had been lifted from the shoulders of the doctors and nurses.

In only six months, medical staff and myself realised that something positive could be done for the patients considered hopeless and 'terminal'. They also saw a change in patients, something that they had not previously seen. This change was usually from a distressed frightened state to a concerned but independent state of mind. Patients felt oppressed and distressed by the rapid deterioration in their physical state. They relied on the medical staff for medical help; but they did not demand of the nurses something that they could not give, as the medical and nursing staff could not give them *time*. The opportunity afforded by my intervention produced a sense of hope in the cancer unit, both providing the necessary psychological support and relief for patients, and allowing medical staff to concentrate on their nursing and medical duties without the burden of guilt.

In my experience, doctors and nursing staff are affected by their work with cancer but conventional training methods do little to help these professionals deal with telling patients about their condition. It is clear that a change in the way cancer patients are perceived in the community and in the hospital might be brought about by a review in the way cancer patients are treated, and this is urgently needed. The presence of a psychoanalytic-orientated therapist working alongside the medical team, someone trained to deal with the more devastating emotional aspects of the disease would have a twofold effect. It would help the patients, by making them feel more whole and integrated, because their feelings about their physical symptoms would find a necessary outlet. It would also provide support and relief for doctors and nurses, who could work co-operatively with the therapist in treating all aspects of the disease.

Terror of losing control

A nurse told me that the wife of one patient, who had cancer of the intestine that had extended into the abdomen wall and was extruding from it, had complained about the problems her husband had sleeping. When her husband returned home from hospital, he sat up all night, afraid that if he went to sleep he would die. On the ward he sat bolt upright in bed and the nurses and doctors did not know how to speak to him. He was very angry. When I first introduced myself he angrily said that he did not need to talk to anyone. Referring to his cancer, he asserted that he was going to 'beat it' on his own. He had refused all sedatives and painkillers because he was convinced that doctors gave them to their patients to make them unconscious before they died. This was regarded as a refusal of treatment and he was left alone. A few days later, he asked to see me and told me of his fear that doctors would try to 'finish him off' with heavy doses of morphia. He was terrified of losing control of his life now that he had cancer.

During several subsequent meetings, he spoke more about this fear. He impressed me as an intelligent, thoughtful man with a broad and sound philosophy of his own. Now that he was ill, he thought that more than ever the onus was on him to take care of his wife and children. But, of course, the nature of the illness meant that he could not. After a few sessions with me, in which he described these fears and anxieties, he was allowed home with a modest amount of sedation, which he could control, and he slept soundly for the first time. The bad internal objects – introjected doctor-figures who wanted him to die without much fuss – had not allowed him to sleep previously. By talking about his fear of losing control, these bad internal objects diminished in power and he was able to regain control of his need to rest.

On one occasion I saw that he had been sketching. He was untutored, but he liked to do it because he found it interesting. It seemed to me that he had an unexplored talent. I gave him a book I had with me by Betty Edwards entitled *Drawing with the Right Side of the Brain*. He had little time left to live but we both regarded this as irrelevant; while it was still possible, life was there to be lived. Again, he felt able to take control. He decided to go into a cottage hospital nearer to his home to make it easier for his family to visit him. Prepared for dying, he changed from being isolated in his anger to being an independent man making decisions for himself and his family without the need for advice or support. I never gave advice and that fact alone changed the politics of his internal world. To his mind, I was someone who introjected him and allowed him to be whatever he was. The transformation of this man from a terrified individual aggressively defending himself against the whole medical establishment to someone who felt integrated and listened to was plain for all on the ward to see. Initially, this patient had confronted the medical staff with a hopeless task. He could not be made 'better', and his cancer could not be removed. My approach was to help him obtain release from the persecutory anxiety that immobilised him and prevented progressive, creative thinking. Without the psychotherapeutic intervention that liberated him, his situation would have been accepted as very painful but inevitable. As the cancer was inoperable, so likewise his mental state was regarded by all around him, including himself, as 'inoperable'.

Using words well

It is ironic that in a cancer hospital – a place where there is abundant evidence of the devastating effect of a few words – scant consideration has been given to the possibility that words can also be used constructively. People can be torn apart by the information they receive but they can also, with the right words, achieve integration – in spite of the fact that their body and the world as they know it is falling apart. The quality of psychoanalytic psychotherapy in the presence of cancer is quite special. It centres on the most important life and death issues without the prevarications of everyday psychotherapy, and it is from the outset seen by cancer patients to be a rare and unique opportunity, to be able to speak freely to someone devoted to listening. There is not, as sometimes occurs in psychoanalysis and psychotherapy with physically healthy people, difficulty in speaking spontaneously and freely about their thoughts. Generally, ill patients are direct in confronting the reality of their illness and are surprisingly eloquent about their feelings. Very little time is needed to produce a dramatic change in the internal world of a patient with cancer. In these circumstances, psychoanalytic psychotherapy becomes an essential life-giving intervention, a high-quality exchange concentrated in a short period of time. This was a revelation to find how much could be accomplished in a limited time.

The contrast between the kind of psychoanalytic psychotherapy applied within a hospital context and that practised by private individuals in return for fees is stark. Two very important differences are the availability of the therapy to any 'ordinary' person (not only to those who can pay) and the transparency of the approach (witnessed on the open hospital ward). In 'classical' psychoanalysis, where two people meet in a room, there is no external assessment made of and to the patient. Anything and nothing can happen between those two people and the entire therapy goes unwitnessed and unevaluated. This is a potentially dangerous set-up. In the hospital, where the therapy happens in a public space, comparisons can be easily made, and there is greater accountability. In dealing with extremely vulnerable individuals, this is vital to good practice.

The psychoanalytic procedure is pre-eminently about 'listening' and is, therefore, unlike other forms of 'talking cure' treatments, such as Cognitive Behavioural Therapy (CBT), which directs and instructs, and aims to change the patient's way of thinking and behaviour. These kinds of therapy tend to generalise about the patient and their problems. Patients are de-individualised and become subjects of cognitive, conditioning, behavioural approaches, which are not concerned with the unconscious of which behaviour is a derivative.

In this chapter, I have described generally how cancer impacts on the individual sufferer, their relatives and the medical carers and professionals within a hospital context, and how it is perceived as something that can destroy all hope and liveliness. The positive and more vital aspects of living with cancer can be mobilised in a very short time, as the pressure put on the end of life leaves the way clear for a creative burst. It is like a bud opening and disclosing its potential flowering. Without a listener, the bud never opens. Sometimes, there is too much going on around the dying patient; people are doing things, asking questions, advising, and chances for reflection and reparation are lost. Such activity generates the idea that the patient is receiving help but, on the contrary, it often overwhelms individuals who needs to do something for themselves, even something no one else can do.

In the next chapter, I describe the different forms of cancer and the effect they have on the individual's conception of his or her own body. The relationship between mental states and an individual's self-perception is explored and the effect of various factors, specifically the anatomical site of cancer, are discussed. I consider the effect of the type of cancer on the individual, whether, for example, it is cancer of the blood or lymphatic system or one of the 'solid' cancers. I consider the way age affects the reaction to cancer, and the way it is particularly devastating for young people to be diagnosed cancer of the genital or reproductive organs. In contrast, I also look at the effect of cancers of the head and neck region, which are detected earlier than cancers inside and away from the head in the body.

Notes

1   S. Sontag, *Illness as Metaphor*, New York: Farrar, Straus & Giroux, 1978, London: Allen Lane, 1979.
2   A. Solzhenitsyn, *Cancer Ward*, trans. N. Bethell and D. Burg, London: Penguin, 1968.
3   J. Bowlby and J. Robertson, 'A Two Year-Old Goes to Hospital', *Psychoanalytic Study of the Child*, 7 (1952), 82–94.
4   Cognitive Therapy is an application of Behaviourism to 'therapy'. The basic concept is that the brain is like a computer and that we are information processors. It embraces concepts from experimental and other scientific approaches to examine how we process information. Cognitive Therapy aims to change the way the patient processes information and it assumes that defects in the information processing produce 'symptoms'. It is in direct contrast to dynamic therapy, which looks at people as people not as computer processors or biological entities.

Chapter 4

Cancer in different areas of the body and mind

The effects of cancer in different parts of the body are due to the significance that different parts of the body have in the brain. In terms of the representation of the body parts on the brain, the face has the greatest significance. On the face, the mouth is the central sensory area, used from the very beginning of life as the means by which the external world is either received or rejected. This area is exquisitely sensitive to touch, taste and smell, and has a bearing on the relationships to other people and sexuality. The self is located in the mouth, principally in the tongue, and cancer in these anatomical regions affects the mind's view of itself. Surgery on the head and neck, for example, is extremely traumatic, because it is an invasion of the most sensitive and vulnerable part of the self. The abhorrence of alien material or living objects is at its most extreme with regards to these areas of the body and the body image. The *idea* of a parasite in these areas produces the most revulsion and distress, and cancer in particular – often perceived as parasitical – precipitates a profound dread of being taken over, and invaded.

In the early stages in the life cycle of a cancer, the aberration of normal cell growth is so small as to be undetectable. At some point the accumulation of cancer cells becomes large enough to signal its presence depending on where it is in the body. At one extreme, a cancer a few millimetres in diameter on a vocal cord produces changes in the voice almost immediately because there is virtually no space and the function of the cord is affected; at the other extreme, a cancer growing in a large space has to be very large before it impinges on structures and affects their function, and cancer of the stomach, pancreas or ovary can be very large before it affects other structures and produces symptoms. The cancer itself produces nothing but cancer cells; symptoms are due to its interference with the normal functioning of various important parts of the body. An individual's awareness of cancer will be immediate when the cancer is visible or is in the sensitive areas of the body whose function is consciously directed.

Cancer of the brain

Cancer of the brain does not produce symptoms that the patient will *recognise* as coming from the brain. The brain and the mind are not consciously connected and symptoms arising because of an interference with function are not related to the brain. Patients have symptoms and are told that they are due to a cancer in the brain or in its vicinity. The symptoms of a brain tumour can be peculiarly frightening because they cannot be understood and the patient feels vulnerable. The first sign may come out of the blue and it is the doctor who relates the signs and symptoms to the brain. The cancer may originate in the brain or come from a primary source elsewhere in the body. In the latter case the patient will know that he or she has cancer and the realisation that it has spread to the brain is disturbing. There are no localising sensations for the patient – it is insidious and silent. The treatment of cancer in the brain by surgery or radiotherapy may affect intellectual functions and personality, but the patient with a brain tumour looks healthy, which is distressing and confusing for relatives and colleagues who expect, but do not receive, that person's normal responses. Appearances are really so important in our relations with other people. Individuals with a brain tumour are caught in a paradox. Because they may look physically normal, they are treated as healthy, whereas in fact they are amputees, except that the effects of the amputation are invisible to others. By contrast, an individual with a deformed face through cancer, is treated, irrationally, as inferior and defective. In the case I outline below, the patient's family suffer also, because after a time when normal responses are not forthcoming, their frustration turns to anger and even contempt. Meanwhile, the patient persists in trying to perform as he did before the operation, oblivious to the changes that have occurred.

Cured cancer, diminished mind

The director of a large business enterprise had a brain tumour successfully removed: there was no recurrence and no effect on bodily functions. He looked the same and, after his operation, he returned to the office believing he could perform as he had done before. The success of his business had depended on his capacity for making rapid decisions, with a good memory for prices and quick responses to market changes. In fact he was incapable of performing like this after his operation, but he persisted, with disastrous consequences. Eventually his embarrassed junior colleagues – with his wife's co-operation – had to prevent him coming into his office. This patient was affable and kindly, always trying to be useful and to prove his competence, but his wife had to watch him continuously. He could not understand why his wife prevented him from doing some things or displayed such anger when he spoiled something. Contempt and anger slowly replaced her pity. She felt that she had no prospect of help, as he did not fall into any defined category of disability. Outside hospital she felt abandoned and alone.

By contrast, when cancer appears in any of the structures surrounding the brain, such as the membranes or the bony structure of the skull, symptoms quickly announce its presence by interference with the function of our most important sense organs: the eye, the ear and the sensitive tongue and vocal chords. The patient is aware of its presence and it may be obvious to other people.

Cancer of the head and neck

These types of cancer can be detected when they are small and can be removed before they have spread to other regions, despite the loss of function that treatment involves. The most common of this type is cancer of the vocal chords; removal of the larynx with the vocal chords renders normal speech impossible but patients who undergo this can and do adapt and many make spirited efforts to learn alternative ways of communicating.

One of the most potent sources of despair is a cancer in this part of the body that continues to grow and spread despite surgery. Surgical extirpation is associated with a loss of some important function – loss of hearing on the affected side when a tumour of the auditory nerve is removed, loss of speech when the larynx or tongue are removed. Normal conversation soon after operation may be impossible for these patients; they can communicate by writing to one other person, but usually not with more than one person, so that they become socially isolated. They also have difficulties with the reactions the condition provokes in others. In the absence of normal speech, for example, many react by speaking loudly or very slowly as they would to a deaf person or someone who is not very intelligent.

In cancer of the head and neck, the disease process is modified by treatment, but it produces problems that are not present before treatment and a price is paid for a possible increase in survival time. A severe handicap due to a form of treatment may spoil life to the point at which it is no longer felt to be worthwhile. Alone, many cannot find a way of surviving treatment and die of despair. Generally, the younger the patient, the greater is the disturbance due to facial disfigurement. Their perception of their status in the world changes as their potential for relationships and career is radically altered by the surgical and medical treatment. Reactions may vary from the complete hopelessness and withdrawal seen in young adults to the cheerful, stoical, pugnacious attitude of mature adults. Despair at any age, however, is more likely to occur when there has been no psychological preparation for the consequences of surgery.

Facial disfigurement

Just as the tongue is exquisitely sensitive to minute alterations in the contours and topography of the teeth and inside the mouth, so the eye is acutely aware of minute fractional changes in the facial musculature – referred to as 'changes of expression'. Foreign objects, particularly living objects like insects, worms and other parasites, have a significance in the mind that varies according to their site in the body. Revulsion, disgust and abhorrence increases the nearer the object is to the mouth and face. The elimination of worms from the anus, for example, has a different effect on the host from worms eliminated from the mouth, as may happen with *Taenia lumbricoides* (a worm that enters the lungs and then, in mature form, is coughed up by the host). Similarly, the sensitivity to interference from outside varies from the relative insensitivity at the back of the mouth and body to the exquisite sensitivity at the front of the mouth and face. Topography is not the only thing to be considered. The significance of a lesion or sensation in an area such as the face can only be determined by finding out how it appears in the inner world of the patient. This will determine the reaction. Someone who is loved because of their own nature will react differently to facial disfigurement than someone who feels themselves to be involved in relationships which are largely dependent on physical transactions and reactions to appearance, especially facial appearance.

Operations on sensitive areas of the body affect in a special way sensitive areas of the psyche. A mastectomy, like a glossectomy (amputation of the tongue) is a simple operation, but both may be regarded as major by the patient with the loss of a sensitive, even sexual, source of pleasure and in the case of the tongue, the loss of speech transforms their social standing and others' reactions. This highlights the need to try to establish before the operation what the patient has in mind, what they see, perceive and apperceive. This should go some way towards distinguishing between imagination and fantasy for both patient and surgeon. The surgeon sees the anatomy but that same anatomy has a different significance in the patient's mind. The loss of a facial feature, for instance, is perceived as a disaster by the patient – a ruination of his or her personal life and a devastation of their social position. The patient's mind centres on the way that the literal loss of face is evidence of his or her reduced, changed standing in other people's minds. This is fantasy. Actually the patient does not know and cannot conceive of what it will be like after the operation. In their imagination, the patient can only say 'I know it (life) will be different, but I do not know how or in what way'. The surgeon knows the facts, but might also have a fantasy of what it feels like to be without a facial feature. The surgeon cannot and does not, however, know anything with certainty. All he or she can do is imagine the various possibilities for the patient. Understanding the potent play of imagination and fantasy could help initiate the process of adjustment to the postoperative situation, and to assist this further, relatives might be involved in the psychotherapeutic process. It is a psychotherapeutic function to differentiate fantasy from reality in the mind of the patient.

Age

Older people with cancer in the head and neck area can be surprisingly stoical about lesions of the face and destructive surgery because they are generally less dependent on superficial appearance and more on character as an estimate of personal worth. With the young person with less character development, the reverse is true. Facial disfigurement may sometimes be borne with unexpected equanimity if the lesions attract the right care and sympathy. Indeed, disfigurement of the facial area may stimulate a response from others that is perceived by the patient as highly supportive and loving. Patients with tinnitus (ringing in the ears), by contrast, suffer, but as no one can see anything it is not always easy for others to appreciate their agony.

In cancer of the head and neck, the surgical procedure, the lesions, and the consequences of the operation should be clearly explained to the patient to remove the possibility of erroneous fantasy and misunderstanding, which arises particularly when people are shocked and frightened. One young woman, the mother of two children, who had part of her jaw removed for cancer of the tongue, was disconcerted to find that on discharge from hospital her husband would not make love to her. It was discovered during an interview with the husband that the reason for this was because he thought that if he kissed her he would be infected with cancer. His fear of infection from her mouth, the vulnerable portal of infection, was irrational and heightened. For him, her mouth, wherein the 'cancer thing' resided, was a part of her to be totally avoided. It was a logical reaction as far as he was concerned, because the cancer had made his wife 'unclean' and therefore not an object of desire. The couple should have been forewarned of this, and it could have been discussed, for the fear of being infected by cancer is not uncommon.

Social difficulties

The paradox with regards to facial disfigurement due to cancer or its treatment is that the cancer itself is less of a threat than the disfigurement and the interference with functions, such as speech, which make social intercourse possible. People are dismayed when they speak to another person and the movements of the face that they anticipate are not forthcoming.

A taxi driver had carcinoma of the larynx and after the larynx was removed he tried to learn oesophageal speech and failed. He then managed to communicate using a vibrator applied to his throat. However, he had to give up his work because he could not reply easily to his passengers. They would speak to him but he could not respond because he was embarrassed to use the monotone mechanical voice of the vibrator. He looked 'normal', but because he could not easily reply to his passengers or explain his dilemma, he sometimes appeared rude. There were times when he would be verbally abused or physically threatened. The cancer was eliminated but the social difficulties ensuing were well nigh insurmountable.

A young man with a successful career as a university lecturer developed cancer of the tongue and, despite a partial excision of the tongue, kept on teaching and lecturing. The cancer recurred and his lecturing had to stop because of the difficulty he had in speaking clearly. He and his wife worked out a plan for his death, but it failed although their arrangements had been carefully made. He now looked 'dumb' and stopped attempting to communicate and became completely unresponsive. The changes were not due to the disease per se but to the hopelessness that had supervened. As with most cases of head and neck cancer, death was not due directly to the disease. No vital functions were interrupted as the cancer spread, but the despair and hopelessness he felt were overwhelming. Such despair, I believe, can be prevented or modified by psychotherapy, and while life will not ultimately be saved, it can be of quality and prolonged.

'Solid' cancers and cancers of the blood and lymphatic systems

Because of their different consequences, a distinction can be made between the cancers that are 'solid', developing from tissues and structures that are solid (such as the lungs, liver, breast and bone), and 'cancers' of the 'glandular' components of the body, which produce blood, lymph or other secretions. The latter do not obtrude into consciousness until there has been a considerable disruption of normal processes and the individual feels ill or when an unusual change is detected, a new lump, for example. An overproduction of lymphocytes, for example, interferes with the production of other cells needed for defence against infection and blood loss and deposits of lymphocytes produce blockages and swellings in different parts. The effect of this kind of cancer is generalised in the body. Some forms develop rapidly, but the cancer cells, being primitive simple cells, are therefore more vulnerable to cell destroyers – chemical toxins and X-rays – and can be eliminated and the condition cured. Other forms are slow growing but more resistant to treatment and this is because the cancer cells are less primitive, more mature, and are more like normal tissue cells.

In young people these diseases can destroy relationships and career prospects. The battle to save life may continue over a long period of time, and may or may not be successful. Meanwhile, they disrupt and limit life for a long time as the treatment is variable and has to be adjusted and frequently repeated, tying the patient to the hospital. The following account is one instance of a family's tribulations when the patient is a child with a form of cancer.

The amazing resources of a child with leukaemia

I was asked to see a 6-year-old boy who was being treated for acute lymphoblastic leukaemia. There was an impasse in his current treatment because he had developed an aversion to taking tablets. All his treatment up to that time had been given in tablet form. The aversion became so extreme that he would vomit if he saw a tablet on television or if he saw his mother take anything in tablet form. He became suspicious of all foods and watched his mother preparing his meals, often refusing to eat if he suspected that his tablets had been put into his food.

His mother asked to see the social worker to discuss the possibility of treatment by hypnosis and readily accepted the suggestion that she discuss her son's eating disorder with me. When I saw the boy, he had been treated with two courses of oral chemotherapy and cerebrospinal irradiation. As he was refusing tablets, treatment had continued to be given by intravenous injection until it became too difficult to find suitable veins. An operation had then been performed to establish an arteriovenous fistula in his leg so that drugs could be given more easily. Unfortunately, this route had become unusable, as the shunt had broken down and apart from oral treatment there was no other way of giving medication.

The father was successful in his profession and, before marriage, the mother had worked with children. It was evident that the parents found it difficult to relate to each other and to their son's illness. They would each ring the ward for advice over different minor matters. Often the ward would have calls from each parent concerning the same problem with requests for messages to be conveyed from one parent to the other by the staff. They were both deeply concerned and disturbed by their son's illness and what he endured seemed at times to be more than they could bear. They suffered separately, however. They appeared to have no resources left for each other and when the little boy was distressed by the side effects of treatment, as happened frequently, his parents were so disturbed that at one point they asked for the treatment to be discontinued. His father said at that time that it would have been better if his son had died when leukaemia was first diagnosed. When the drugs were changed and there were fewer side effects they were palpably relieved.

I met the mother and the patient, usually accompanied by his younger sister, on the children's ward. There were small cubicles so that the patient and his sister could play while I spoke to the mother in a cubicle. Her husband was too busy to accompany her on most visits to the hospital. When I was with the patient he looked into the room but did not come in. I told him that I would be bringing a case with toys in it for our next meeting and I would see him on his own. He was pleased at the prospect and came eagerly to our appointment and played freely with the toys, building structures that were delicate and finely balanced. I intended seeing him regularly and he was intrigued at having a special time with me and a case of toys that would not be used by anyone else.

One day I came with this case of toys and instead of opening it straight away as usual he asked me very quietly to go and talk to his mother. I left him with playing with the toys and went with his mother to another cubicle. Her face was bruised and she said that she and her husband had quarrelled violently. She had lost her temper with her son and her husband had then railed at her for behaving in this way with him. This had led to physical violence with their two children as onlookers. Her anger with her son was an expression of her frustration with his illness.

I began sessions for several weeks with the mother and after a while I started seeing the father. After my first few sessions with his parents the patient began spontaneously to take his medicine in tablet form again. I surmised, or observed, that he now controlled the situation and he had in a sense brought his mother for treatment. She now demonstrated how much she cared for him by staying with the psychotherapy. Before that, his refusal of oral medication was an expression of his despair at his mother's tantrums, which appeared to him to be because of the inconvenience his illness caused her. She was not the mother to whom he could turn for solace, to assuage his pain – she was preoccupied by her own pain.

When the arteriovenous fistula operation was performed on him (a response to being unable to take anything by mouth), he was passive. He was not asked if he wanted it and the procedure was not explained to him. His feelings were of no account; he was being treated to make others feel better. When the fistula became unusable he was back in control, because without his agreement tablets or injections could not be used. He was empowered. His vomiting, a rejection of treatment, was his demonstration of his need to be free, and considered as a human being. It was his way of drawing his parents' attention to the needs of their children.

The parents' feuding had excluded the children. With surprising insight and intelligence, this boy manoeuvred his mother into a meeting with what was supposed to be his therapist to display the black eye, advertising the physical violence that both he and his sister had witnessed. She was unable to avoid the confrontation and the offer of help when her son was watching. She came from a violent family background and with little provocation had explosive rages. On many occasions during the psychotherapy she would in other circumstances have been enraged and walked away but she felt 'contained' in psychotherapy by the reality of her son accepting treatment from the moment that she accepted this help for herself. She attended regularly for her psychotherapy sessions and the family dynamics changed.

They continued to develop during the following years despite the vicissitudes of a family dominated by the disease; there were crises, relapses and reprieves until the final visit to the hospital.

After seven years there was no more treatment possible. He was 13 and had survived longer than any other child at that time with leukaemia. He sat propped up in bed in a single room; he was alert – taking in everything around him. His parents and his sister sat by his bed looking up to him, no one speaking. Had psychotherapy not been available the story would have been different; one significant effect was that it enabled his physical treatment to continue. In this instance the child patient became resourceful and looked after others who conventionally could have been his exemplars.

This child became amazingly wise and courageous in the face of his illness. He matured and, to my knowledge, never complained and accepted death when it came at the end. In the act of comforting and supporting his family, he taught us all a great deal. He was more adult in a sense than most of the adults around him.

Cancer in the young

Cancer affecting the blood or lymphatic system is common among younger adults. Such cancers are characterised by either a very rapid deterioration or a prolonged course with many remissions and relapses, and many changes of treatment. When treatment ceases to be effective after a long period of varying fortunes there is a peculiarly painful dilemma. The patient is active and alert, living at home, invariably aware of their physical state and knowing that the doctors have nothing further to offer. Until the rapid and complete failure of all body systems they can only wait. This is a terrible and lonely position to be in and very distressing to the young doctors or nurses who identify with the patient who feels condemned without any form of comfort or solace. Anticipating this final dilemma, doctors referred young patients to me when further treatment was impossible. There were always special problems associated with these patients because of their age and situation.

The distress of a young couple

A young married couple in their early twenties asked for help, as they were both distressed by their situation. He had a form of leukaemia that had been diagnosed twelve months previously. Since then they had lived with her parents while he had treatment, which involved periods in hospital and outpatient appointments that were so irregular that they said they spent a large part of their time hanging around the hospital. Consequently, they were unable to make plans and have a life of their own. He was deteriorating but as the treatment was often debilitating the couple were inclined to attribute his weakness to this rather than the disease. How much he had deteriorated was brought home to them when they saw on television a film about the hospital's leukaemia unit. It had been made several months previously and he had been one of the patients filmed when he had had a marrow transplant. They were shocked to see how much he had changed since that time, when his hair had been normal and he had a beard. He was now completely hairless and emaciated. They felt abandoned because the film dealt in a light-hearted way with the unit's efficiency and statistics and the doctors simply enthused about percentages and the survival rates for treatments. He realised that to the doctors he was no more than a statistic, and that as an individual he did not exist. For him and his wife treatment had been a 'hundred per cent failure'. The hospital had become for him a concentration camp, because no one cared about him now. Not only did they feel terribly isolated and helpless but they felt that their trust had been betrayed. When the treatment was to be whole body radiation, for example, he had asked for a shield for his testicles only to be told that he was already sterile from the drugs he had received. This was a terrible shock. The couple felt that had they known this they could have delayed the treatment just long enough to conceive or store semen.

Doctors, who were mostly the same age as the patient, displayed an astonishing lack of concern. He never showed signs of *responding* to their treatment. Not only was he not gratifying and rewarding by getting better, he was a reproach and a problem, for which they had no solution. Unwittingly, all the people who had been in contact with this young couple had made the unit a torture chamber. He had been, in effect, castrated – rendered infertile and impotent – and this meant they could not have children. They felt they had been tricked and were now sinking into despair as he faced decline and death with no hope of offspring. No one had warned him of these consequences of the treatment or explained how it occurred so that he could have been involved in decisions affecting their lives. It was as if he was the victim of persecution who had been cruelly treated.

He was physically weak and looked so pitiable that he believed his wife found him unattractive. She was single-minded and supported him and by involving him in making decisions helped him to regain his self-respect. Their world had turned upside-down and their hopes for the future seemed to be destroyed, but he was awarded a place on a university course starting four months after treatment started. This was a mixed blessing, because while they both knew that he was not getting better they were given university accommodation, but this was only as long as he was able to study. The woman did everything she could to minimise his feelings of impotence and inferiority. Because the drugs and the disease affected his potency and he could not make love to her, he feared his wife would cease to love him. She was quick to reassure him that their sexual relationship was not at this time important to her.

Young patients like these have no resources and their parents, because their children have left home, may have moved to a smaller home with very limited accommodation. These young patients on the verge of being adult and independent have a miserable time. In this instance a young woman made a brave effort to make her partner feel precious and valued, but society tends to transmit a soul-destroying message to such patients: 'No one wants to see you again! You are no longer of interest to us and we are not concerned with what will happen to you now'. Often this is made quite explicit in the medical notes, such as 'there is nothing more that we can do', 'further appointments would not serve any useful purpose'.

Missing something

A patient was sent to me by the social worker at the sister hospital, the Royal Marsden at Sutton. He was obviously very ill and his wife was on the verge of tears. He told me that he had Hodgkin's disease (cancer of the lymph glands) and that it had started two and a half years previously. His brother had had the same disease and it had been treated successfully. The patient was studying for a PhD, living in university accommodation for married couples. He said that he had no idea why he had been sent to me and then said that he had considered it shameful for them to have to have a psychiatrist helping them.

The couple did not want to see a psychiatrist because the patient's wife had had a breakdown through being unable to cope with their circumstances and had already been referred for psychiatric treatment. After her experience, she did not want to see another. She said that the psychiatrist had refused to let her go – contacting her work place to keep in touch with her – and she had had to leave her work because she was so ashamed of being pursued in this way.

The couple described an awful situation with their flat: the toilet would get blocked, plumbers would come and make a terrible mess, which they had to clear up, and then it would block again. When the toilet was blocked the patient was afraid to use it and he became constipated. Because of his treatment he was vomiting frequently, so it was an unpleasant situation. During this time the patient had a succession of treatments, none of which appeared to be working. He was on one treatment that he expected would cause him to lose his hair, but the effects of the chemotherapy were so awful that he discontinued it before the course had been completed.

The last time I saw him it was an emergency. He was in hospital and staff thought he was going to die. The social worker said that the junior doctor had told his wife, who at first appeared not to know anything and then broke down and said that she had known it all along. I saw the patient and we discussed his situation. There was a cruel irony here because after all their trouble with accommodation they had just been given a very nice flat, which he had plans to furnish. He was usually irascible but on this occasion he was friendly and said he was glad to see me. He had not expected to see me again as had happened with other doctors. His main concern was what his wife would do when he had gone – he feared that she might commit suicide – but he felt reassured by the possibility that she could get help and, judging by her response to the few sessions that she had already had, she would derive benefit from it.

The man said that he regretted that his life was limited and that he would not have children. This sentiment is not peculiar to those suffering from cancer, but in his case he had a fantasy that he was 'missing' something that others had. In fact he did not know what he was missing, and through talking, the futility of such 'regrets' was made apparent. A distinction between fantasy and reality was drawn; the 'others' to whom he attributed everything that was on the side of life, leaving himself feeling empty, persecuted him.

The thought that this patient was missing something is a fantasy about the past. He does not know what would have happened if he had taken a different path. He 'sees', in the transitive sense, all the good things in others, and is left feeling empty by comparison. He is persecuted. Fate has picked on him to be empty and bereft, while others have everything. This fantasy can happen at any time to anybody in any condition.

As noted above, the cancers that affect the blood and lymphatic system usually have a long history, with periods of illness alternating with periods of remission. As a result, the effect on the patient and their relatives is different from the situation with many other forms of cancer. The effects are prolonged and living with the emotional ups and downs takes its toll on relationships. The patient is often alert and aware of their situation until the very last hours of their life. With older patients, the illness can hang over them like a sword of Damocles. In many cases it is the partner of the patient who breaks down and asks for help. Some patients asked for psychological help, but the majority were unable to do so or did not think that their doctors would be concerned with their non-physical problems. In my experience, psychotherapeutic help was always needed when young patients were involved in long and testing treatment. What transpired was usually a psychoanalytically informed group procedure, the couple constituting a group.

Cancer of the genital and the urine/excretory systems

The genital and the urine/excreting areas of the body have a different psychological significance for men and women. The penis functions to eject urine and is handled by adults for this purpose many times in the day. It is also a sex organ when arousal and erection occur. The scrotum is external and sensitive. Cancer and surgical treatment in these areas is profoundly disturbing because of their psychological significance and the role these parts of the body play in sexual and reproductive functions. Other organs involved in sexual activity and excretion, such as the prostate gland and the bladder, are not on the surface of the body and cancer in them may not be detected at such an early stage. In women, the organs most frequently affected are internal, and include the ovaries, the cervix or the uterus, and the fallopian tubes, and as with male internal organs, cancer may develop without signalling its presence for some time. Cancers affecting the vagina, labia and clitoris are disturbing, however small, because these areas are sensitive and continuously attended to in excretion and in sexual activity. Cancer affecting the genitalia can be detected early and is not an immediate threat to life but it nevertheless changes the patient's life forever. Again, the younger the patient, the more disturbing is the effect. The patient who has cancer of the penis, for example, may not feel ill but has to choose between either surgical treatment that will eradicate the cancer, or living with the spreading cancer.

In the following case, my intervention acted as a catalyst for emotional relief that would not otherwise have been possible. It is not only an illustration of a very ill patient caring for a spouse, but also of the power of psychological forces to override physical deterioration. The devotion and determination of a patient plumbs resources that sustain life against all odds, even when the failure of all body systems seems to have occurred.

Coping with castration

A young man had cancer in his penis. The surgeon said told him that there was no alternative way of eliminating the cancer other than by removal of the penis and testicles. Without the operation, the cancer would continue to spread, and he would die. The surgeon asked me to see if there was any way in which the patient could be helped to make his decision. The patient was weeping as he told me about the surgery and his despair at what it entailed. He said he would never be able to make love again, and could not bear being without a penis and testicles – that is, not a complete man. What would other men think and what would his wife feel? In our sessions he was full of despair, and there was nothing that I could say that could reduce the pain and anguish. He was also bitter, because when he had first complained of symptoms proper notice had not been taken of them. He believed that because he was a young man he was misdiagnosed. It was assumed that his problem consisted of a venereal infection and he was given inappropriate treatment. The chance of very early treatment for the cancer had been lost.

During this difficult time, however, his wife had conceived and by the time I saw him, they had a baby. The man decided to have the operation – his decision was made suddenly – but afterwards he was very distressed, with no clear idea how he was going to manage. At one point, he felt suicidal but was held back from acting on this impulse because of the baby and the considerable strength and determination of his wife. Our sessions afforded him the opportunity to give voice to his thoughts, to work through the feelings engendered by this particular form of cancer and its impact on his masculinity. One can only speculate as to what would have happened had he not had this opportunity, but the sessions provided containment of feelings of conflict and distress, and permitted him to stand back and evaluate his position as a husband and father with responsibilities in a more detached way. Without psychotherapy, I think the decision to have the operation would have been the same but there would probably have been a much more intense and longer period of grief after the operation.

The cancer may be removed in young people but many possibilities are also removed and, both before and after surgery, a lot of time and work is required to enable the patient to work through the powerful destructive feelings. Patients react quite differently to the loss of function that castration entails. A 30-year-old married man developed cancer in one testicle and both testes had to be removed. He and his wife did not have any children and although this did not appear to be his main concern at first, after the operation he became explosively aggressive at the slightest provocation. This resulted in several physical attacks on other car drivers and his wife found it impossible to live with him. Psychotherapy before his operation would have given him the opportunity to work out what would happen and dispel the ubiquitous fantasies about manhood and male competitiveness related to the genitals. He was a victim of projective identification acted out violently. He felt emasculated and inferior to 'other people' and perceived everybody looking at him in this way. These 'other people' in his mind were like a gang sneering and condescending. After his wife left him, he returned to the hospital and asked for help because he realised that he was losing his family and his friends. He was unable to control his aggressiveness and to understand what was going on in his mind but, through the sessions, he understood that he felt he was worthless and, in order to cope with this, he attributed these ideas to other people in his mind. From the therapy, he gained some insight and relief from his feelings of inferiority and realised that his worth and quality as a man was not affected by surgery.

So far, I have outlined some of the salient features of cancer in different areas of the body and the way in which they are perceived in the mind. Psychotherapy should be sensitive to the particular issues arising from the different locations of cancer in and on the body and its effects on the self-perception and social interaction. Where social functions are impaired, in cancer of the head and neck, for example, careful attention to issues of isolation and ostracisation should be considered. Where the sexual functions are disrupted or obliterated, special attention should be paid to the patient's close relationships and feelings about being emasculated or de-feminised. In the following sections, I focus on gynaecological cancer and the particular trauma engendered by this for women.

The weal of gynaecological cancer

Research on the effects of gynaecological cancer, particularly that which is concerned with what is termed 'the quality of life', is invariably statistical and quantitative. For example, in assessing the effect on sexual enjoyment and behaviour, coitus and its frequency are used as an indication of sexual satisfaction or dissatisfaction. But 'satisfaction' is not necessarily related to 'orgasmic frequency' and the quality of love and intimacy is not necessarily related to this crude assessment of sexual behaviour. The quality of a woman's whole life when she has gynaecological cancer has to be considered in relation to what it was before she became ill. For example, a very unsatisfactory relationship prior to the illness can be transformed for the better by a couple having to cope with the cancer. In other circumstances, a very poor relationship between a man and a woman may just simply continue to be poor, devoid of intimacy and affection.

The effect on the male partner

The effect of gynaecological cancer on the male partner is rarely considered and close enquiry may be required to elicit difficulties here. With skilled intervention a deteriorating situation may be salvaged, fondness and love being restored and intensified in the presence of vicissitude to become fulfilling in a way that they never have experienced before. Some men become impotent in one way or another as a reaction to their partner's cancer. This may be apparent rather than real in that the man may be afraid to make sexual approaches, because he views his partner as being damaged. He may be appalled at gynaecological procedures, their indelicacy and invasiveness and he may fear that any sexual approach will be viewed by his partner as a male assault. However, working out a relationship against the background of serious illness and treatment may enable the man and the woman to change the way they regard one another, for the better. The man can be encouraged to serve his partner, attending to her needs and demonstrating what his feelings for her are (demonstrating something perhaps that could not be put into words). He can be encouraged to treat his partner as a precious object. His sexual behaviour can become the 'love-making' part of serving and caring for her. The frequency of sex and orgasm are no indications in men or women of the burgeoning regard and respect they may develop for one another.

The effects of gynaecological cancer

A complementary approach to patients with gynaecological cancer is absolutely fundamental to their care. Cancer in this region of the body is not a mere matter of mechanical malfunction, but affects the mind, personal relationships, and the individual's sense of well-being. It is an area complexly bound up with the emotional essence of life. Gynaecological cancer is the loss of a health-giving activity. Physical and physiological changes occur *pari passu* with profound effects on the mind. The removal of parts of the genitalia is the loss of the means whereby the most powerful physical expression of love can occur.

As gynaecology patients are all women with developmental epochs unique to women, a psychoanalytic psychotherapist would have to appreciate women's attitudes to the menarche, menopause, menstruation and fertility. In the younger age group, gynaecological cancer may require treatment that itself produces sterility. If a patient is single this may affect her current or future relationships or even her marriage prospects. With pre- or postmenopausal women with cancer, different considerations apply according to their situation maritally, sexually and with regard to progeny. The treatment of gynaecological cancer, in such cases, may produce an enforced and premature menopause removing free choice with regard to having children and sexual activity. This can seriously affect the woman's relationship with others – to her partner, to other women, to her family. She may feel inadequate as a woman.

The gynaecological anatomical region is psychologically very special, being exquisitely sensitive and primary in sexual arousal. A 'malignancy', something 'bad', in this region is especially disturbing and significantly different in its effects from cancers in other parts of the body. It affects the body image – its reflection in the mind. Surgical and radiological treatments invade and expose these private parts. Reactions will vary according to fantasies and feelings of the individual woman about her genitalia prior to developing cancer. Ideally, the psychotherapist should be familiar with these issues and be able to present individual variations to the gynaecologist who is planning treatment.

The psychoanalytic psychotherapist should be experienced in dealing with sexual problems in women, as well as appreciating male reactions to them in the context of gynaecological treatment. With limited time and restricted opportunities, the psychotherapist may have to conduct short-term, flexible yet intensive psychotherapy interviews, attending to the exigencies of the inner world of the patient, while she may be buffeted by the toxic and destructive assaults coming from outside in the form of the 'treatment of the cancer' (as opposed to 'treating the self'). She may fall between two stools if she sees a psychotherapist who is not familiar with the physical situation and does not take it into account – because other doctors may assume that all is being taken care of and they can continue to treat without considering what the patient feels during treatment. On both fronts, therefore, the patient can feel misunderstood and unworthy of a proper hearing.

A change of heart

I was referred a patient who was undergoing treatment for ovarian carcinoma. She had an unhappy background and during her description of her husband's behaviour since she had become ill, she realised that her husband was homosexual and some of their problems had been a consequence of this and not due to her. She had two sons at a very good expensive private school. The marriage had been characterised by her husband's violence towards her and his failure to respect and act with tenderness. He always took her to his company dinners but never introduced her to his many friends. They had not had sexual intercourse for five years. They were the same age but she looked so much younger than her husband that people thought that he had married a much younger woman. Both his parents had been physically violent towards her when she stayed with them. Her own family disapproved of the marriage because of the religious differences. Her family religion did not accept converts and she had to marry within the religion. It appeared that she had been a victim of abuse and persecution coming from all sides, particularly from her husband. When she was undergoing treatment, her husband changed and could not have been more considerate and kind to her. In the early phase of treatment when it appeared that she was improved, he would revert to his unpleasant behaviour towards her. She said that she had to talk to someone about this and began to think of what action she should take. She wanted now to leave the marriage; although he changed when she was ill and would attend to her when she was incontinent, she did not think that he did this out of love for her but because of his homosexuality. A certain insight developed in the course of the psychotherapy sessions and although very ill she was able to express her desire to be liberated from what had been a restrictive and demeaning relationship. She felt freer and regained a measure of self-respect for the first time since she had been married.

Unlike other non-gynaecological patients, these patients invariably know the diagnosis whether explicitly told or not. They also have an irrational feeling of failure and worthlessness. They may often be self-effacing and almost invariably say that they feel sorry for their male partner and what they deem to be his poor bargain in the relationship (i.e. his sexual deprivation). The families of such patients often show surprising reactions. Frequently, children react to their mother's illness with cruel demands, as if they cannot stand the idea of losing their mother, and so they refuse to accept that she is ill and weakened and make inordinate demands of her to keep up their routines. However, in a large proportion of cases the male partner is supportive.

Cervical cancer

One patient, suffering from cancer of the cervix, was surgically treated by the removal of the ovaries, uterus and vagina. The spread of the disease continued, however, and the patient was told that she had only a few months remaining. Her son was in the care of the local authority, because of her alleged maltreatment of him. The man she was now living with was devoted to her and, although not the father of her son, supported her whilst she tried to regain custody of her son. Before she died, she felt urgently that it was necessary to regain some dignity and to redress the situation, so that her son could appreciate her and realise that she loved him and did not want to get rid of him. She wanted to feel that she would be remembered by him with affection. Against the background of inexorable physical decline she mobilised help through a course of psychotherapy and fought a legal battle to regain her son. She was the dominant person in the household and despite the impossibility of sexual intercourse, which had been important in their relationship, her male partner remained by her side devotedly during the last months of her life.

If doctors and nurses associated with gynaecological cancer patients only see patients who become moribund, usually in the period before dying, they may take this ending to be commonplace and unavoidable. When the whole situation takes a different course, the effect on nursing staff in particular is quite startling, and they are invariably relieved to find that the ending can be different from what they expected. Many nurses that I met were distressed to realise that they had been associated only with painful endings. They thought there was no alternative, and some of them felt that they could not go on being a party to such distress while at the same time being unable to affect changes in the care and treatment of patients. Unfortunately, some sensitive nurses with a strong sense of vocation left the profession.

Many of the features that distinguish gynaecological cancer from other forms of cancer also apply to breast cancer. It is similar, because of the way it features in reproduction and in sexual behaviour and is virtually a 'woman's disease'. It rarely occurs in males and where it does it does not have the same significance sexually and in appearance.

Last-minute volte-face

A 50-year-old woman had cancer of the breast for one year before drawing attention to it; by then it was large and fungating and there were secondary deposits in her spine which affected her legs. Palliative physiotherapy did not improve her mobility but she set great store by it and said that she believed it would cure her. She was unpleasant to the nursing staff, being always demanding and insidiously disruptive by complaining privately about the nurses to her own consultant. In psychotherapy, she repeatedly affirmed that she believed her loss of function in her legs was temporary. She protested vehemently that even if others were not certain, she was going to recover and she cited as proof of this the fact that it was thought worthwhile to give her physiotherapy.

I saw this patient regularly and did not collude with her denial of her condition. I would point out the reality. She could not walk and it was only her insistence that persuaded the physiotherapist to continue. It was made clear to her by the physiotherapist that she could not improve her situation but at the insistence of the patient continued to give her some physiotherapy. I saw her regularly and I saw her as an intelligent woman refusing to admit that her condition was irremediable and to discuss the reality with her husband and son.

I interpreted her wish to control the cancer and everyone in her life, the Sister and nurses in particular, by projecting all the badness outside herself into the nurses. After each session she would smile as I left and benignly say goodbye. Her position was maintained and she had the consultant, her husband and son and the nurses controlled and frightened of her. I was not frightened and was undeterred from referring to her death and the opportunity she now had to make arrangements with her family. How did she want to leave them? What feelings about her did she want them to have? She would insist that this was irrelevant because she was not going to die.

Just two days before she died there was a dramatic transformation in her demeanour. She became sad and kindly and took pains to seek out individual nurses that she had maligned, apologising for the difficulties she had created and confessing that she had known all along there was no hope that she would recover from the cancer. The Sister in charge was particularly moved and deeply affected by this *volte-face*. Having seen that such a transformation was possible with psychotherapy, she became convinced of the value of treating patients in a more holistic way. Nursing, in her view, was an essentially holistic task, and proper treatment of patients who would not recover from cancer involved attending to their psychological state.

A devoted couple

In the case of a young married woman, the cancer was in the genito–urinary region and had developed from cancer of the cervix. She had been transferred to a ward referred to, at that time as the 'terminal ward' – a name that was subsequently changed. Transfer to this ward meant that active treatment had ceased and this was often underlined by the absence of the usual visiting of the patient by the medical team. The woman was receiving large amounts of morphia, at her insistence, by intramuscular injection. She lay on her bed looking as if she was dying but when I spoke to her and asked her what was happening to my surprise she responded not by describing her physical state but began by telling me about her husband. She thought that her husband would not manage without her, that he would be unable to fend adequately for himself in negotiations with their employer (they were employed as a couple with accommodation being provided). She was afraid that after she died her husband would lose his job and have nowhere to live. She also feared that without her he would commit suicide. She wanted to go home and negotiate with their employer so that her husband had both accommodation and work after she died. She had no need to be in bed at this time; she was still physically quite active and energetic but she was convinced that without morphia she would suffer. She felt that morphia was sustaining her and would only do so if it was given in hospital by intramuscular injection. She was terrified of going home because she would have to rely on the District Nurse and she was afraid that she would not be able to get to her regularly.

In view of the very advanced state of her cancer I surmised that she would need morphia very shortly in any event, and she concurred with this. She was not actually in much pain but it was something she desperately clung to perhaps as a support. When she was reassured that the District Nurse would be forewarned of her anxieties about receiving regular injections, she went home for a weekend. Subsequently, she went home for a much longer period the arrangement being that she could return to hospital when it suited her. For over a week, during this longer time at home she managed without having the morphia injections. She successfully negotiated with their employer so that her husband's position and accommodation were secure and guaranteed to continue after her death. She was now alert and quite unlike the picture that she first presented. She still felt concerned about her husband and his ability to cope after she died.

This woman told me about her main concerns. The first was her husband's future when she was gone. Her husband was distraught at his wife's condition. He was obviously deeply in love with her. She was the more direct and executive of the two. He admired her and was immensely moved by her devotion to him. He said that he could not envisage living without her, and I interpreted this as meaning that he would not want to live without her. He nodded and said he was anticipating the desolation and thinking of suicide after she died.

I spoke to him about her wishes for him and how she would live on in his mind. He could keep her in mind by thinking about what she would do in certain circumstances and what she had done. I put it to him that his wife – as he knew her – would be devastated to think that she was the cause of his death, but more importantly, that his suicide would mean that her life had been worthless, leaving nothing behind. He wept bitterly but promised that he would not kill himself. He was beginning a life of mourning. He benefited from the psychotherapy sessions. They gave him the space to grieve but they also helped him to become stronger and more positive in caring for his wife, to the point that she no longer had any doubt that he would be able to take care of himself after she was gone.

After what proved to be her last period at home she returned to the ward and asked to see me. She was fully dressed when we met on the ward and looked quite unlike a patient on her bed about to die. She told me without preamble that she was now going to die – and said, 'everything is blocked'; she could not even pass urine. The cancer of her cervix, which was widespread when I had first spoken with her, had spread even further. Her pelvis was solid with cancer. She had survived against all expectations, and at this last meeting she was taking her leave and with great dignity and strength she showed me how independent she was and how proud she was of what she had achieved. The strength of will manifest when she was freed to act as she wished enabled her to carry on living, despite being at death's door.

The medical assumption was that this patient's miserable state was a response to her hopeless physical state. In effect, she was less concerned about her physical state than its impact on others after her death. She felt isolated and, through psychotherapy, had the opportunity to solve the personal problems that were more crucial to her than the cancer. The strength of her love and character were quite impressive and it was brought to the fore powerfully in the brief psychotherapy. It is a tragic situation when a patient dies with so many personal issues unresolved and with feelings of helplessness and hopelessness. It is an unnecessary situation, especially when something constructive can be done through words because it means that an unnecessary burden can be lifted.

This woman typifies the personal growth that can occur through psychotherapy. She was transformed from a terrified, ostracised, oppressed woman, waiting for death alone. Virtually no one spoke about her feelings. They anticipated them and then avoided them because they felt they had nothing helpful to say. She felt that no one in hospital was interested in talking to her because her death was certain. Doctors and nurses could not alter that fact, but they could not treat her sense of hopelessness because it mirrored their own. For the medical staff, her withdrawn demeanour before psychotherapy was regarded as 'normal' and commonplace, but they were in considerable denial in her case. The thought of speaking to her at length and exploring her feelings was frightening to the nurses. Her background and her relationships were largely unknown to them and the general assumption was that dying alone and miserable was the standard way in which life ends. In general, nurses do not speak to such patients because they feel they have nothing to say which would make the situation better, but by not saying anything, they perpetuate the fantasy that there is no hope, that life is over. Though the husband was sad and bereaved after her death, he was able to fulfil her expectations of him and found the strength to live on. From a position of apparent despair, she proved herself to be an exceptional person with considerable resources.

In this chapter, I have touched on two issues pertinent to the treatment of cancer patients – pain and truth. It is often assumed that adequate treatment for all types of cancer is about physical pain relief, but in my experience this is a complex issue because psychological pain can produce difficulties that can affect physical survival chances. The issue of the truth is one that affects both medical staff and patients. So often, the truth of a patient's condition is concealed from them and this can have devastating consequences for the individual and their ability to cope with the thought of dying. In the two chapters following, I discuss the issues of pain and truth, and argue that unless a complementary approach to pain is achieved, and unless proper, truthful attention is paid to understanding the suffering of a patient with cancer, then we are not helping that individual to live up to their potential for as long as they have to live. The responsibility of the medical and psychological support is to work together in making sure that the patient is treated with respect. Understanding the precise nature of the pain and how it is perceived is a crucial and vital intervention. Pain, as I will argue in the next chapter, is not always relieved by the administration of palliative drugs, because the significance of pain in the mind and other psychological changes determine what ensues.

Chapter 5

Mind-bending pain

The topic of pain relief is a popular one and it is often claimed that the main problem that arises for cancer patients is that of adequate or inadequate pain relief or control. The terms 'pain relief' and 'pain control' have become so commonplace they are now jargon, and there is the assumption that they refer simply to the physical condition of patients. It was common for patients to be sent to me because they were complaining of pain and discomfort. All the measures that had been taken to relieve the pain and discomfort had been of no avail. After a time, however, when the patient had become engaged and interested in the psychotherapy sessions, the pain frequently ceased to be an issue. It may have still been present, but the patient's attention was directed to other preoccupations and considerations. The pain ceased to be disruptive, and it was suffered and relegated to the background of the patient's attention.

On the other hand, if the patient was bored, lying in a hospital bed for many hours without interruption or companionship, not only might the pain and discomfort have been the sole focus of his attention, but it became the point of communication between the patient and the staff. Often it was the only way in which a discussion with medical attendants could be initiated. Mentioning pain on a ward round or in outpatients produced something doctors and nurses were attracted to dealing with, and it stood in contrast to questions about their own and the patient's attitude to physical deterioration and death.

This chapter is divided into two main themes, one theoretical and the other practical. In the first part, I discuss the theory that pain and sensory suppression at a conscious level can occur. In hospital, the psychological dimension of pain often goes untreated while the physiological aspects are met with drugs. I argue that a complementary approach is needed, that is, an approach that assesses both the patient's perception of their illness – and the fear and despair they might have about being seriously ill – and the patient's physical condition. In the second part of the chapter, I discuss this approach with specific reference to cancer patients, and what it means to 'control' the pain (both the physical and psychological pain) of cancer.

Remembering the experience of pain

Let us start with a practical yet philosophical example. If I have to perform a simple surgical operation, for example I incise a breast to a depth of 3–4 centimetres for an abscess or I reduce a misalignment of bones in a fractured arm, it is generally accepted that without an anaesthetic these procedures would involve unacceptable pain. If we were to hold the patient still, as in the pre-anaesthetic era, and proceed despite fear and pain, the trauma would leave a scar. The patient would indeed remember the occasion – but despite the tears and screams would not be able to recall and reproduce in imagination the pain as they would the visual experience. They could, if asked, see again in the 'mind's eye' their bedroom, a beach, the road they live in – in great detail. Some may even visualise a scene to furnish forgotten details. Eidetic imagery is even more detailed and vivid but is rare in adults. We may use words in describing the event but we cannot recreate in our mind the physical sensations.

The physical sensations have not disappeared. They are recorded somewhere because they can return uncalled for, with great vividness. For example, after a rough sea journey our body may still feel the swaying and pitching of the boat on dry land. However, if surgical procedures that are usually painful are carried out without using an anaesthetic to produce unconsciousness or numbness and the patient is urged to focus their attention on a visual image, with the suggestion that, as they do so they will become unaware of the other physical sensations – then they will not feel pain when the surgical operation is performed. They will not recall feeling pain and will not behave as if the experience was unpleasant. They appear calm and relaxed.

As one speaks to such a patient the truth – the neuropsychological and psychological truth – is immediately demonstrable. One may point out that they do not feel the hardness of the trolley on their back, or their shoes on their feet until they are mentioned, as they attend to what is being said to them. After such an experience a patient may say they do not even recall the operation – and appear surprised that it has been completed. If the patient is asked in a random way what comes to mind they may then describe the procedure. They may have felt the scalpel cutting the skin – the manipulation – but no pain. This pain seems to be in a special relation to memory different from other sensations that can be recalled in imagery.

Pain is not experienced as part of consciousness, it displaces the usual experience of consciousness and then there is no 'pain image'.

Experience of pain in the present

We use the words in everyday language as if it were possible to 'imagine' a past experience of pain. We remember the time and the place and can label the experience as horrible, dreadful, unpleasant, but it is not reproducible. Pain is therefore a present experience and while the reaction to it may be remembered, the pain itself is not reproducible. We cannot say, for example as we would about a visual experience, 'I can picture it vividly', and go over it in our mind. In many situations when the attention is distracted pain is not felt – as occurs, for example, in battle and in emergencies. The Accident Room and the Operating Theatre are drama-filled settings and it is the drama that is visualised rather than the pain; hence the ease with which otherwise painful and frightening procedures can be performed without having to induce unconsciousness with anaesthetic agents.

The continued experience of pain depends upon change – coming and going – each return of pain being a pain anew. This is what is usually meant by the term 'chronic pain'. Fluctuation in intensity and/or changes in quality must occur for it to be present in consciousness. A process may initiate pain but the pain will cease to be experienced if there is no change – a process of attenuation occurs.

Different perceptions of pain

We may now consider the 'perception' of pain. A stimulus that is thought to herald death or irreversible damage would produce fear. The sensation would then be described as very unpleasant. In other words, we describe and feel pain according to its significance. A stimulus can be perceived in different ways – a pinprick, if it is thought to be harmless may produce a wince but nothing more, but if it were perceived as heralding dissolution (if it were, say, the poisoned tip of an assassin's umbrella), it would produce a different reaction. This is a factor varying the reactions of patients with cancer to a pain stimulus. The pain may fluctuate, thus maintaining its ascendancy in attention but in addition it is 'agonising' and 'fearsome' because it portends something worse – more disintegration and more dreaded pain – 'dreaded' pain being pain perceived as destroying equanimity and integrity. Often there is confusion and great fear based on fantasy and they may be construed as indicating great pain.

Apperception

In some laboratory experiments, where the individuals waited alone in a recording room for the doctor to arrive, it was noticed that there was a marked increase in heart rate and blood pressure and psychogalvanic skin responses (these are ways of recording the skin resistance and its sensitivity to emotional changes) to sounds of doors closing on the corridor prior to the experimenter entering the room. After the doctor had entered the room the same sound stimulus did not produce any of these responses. The patient anticipating entry of the experimenter into the room gave the door noises a significance they did not have after he was installed in the room. We might refer to these phenomena as 'apperception'. The stimulus is 'perceived' but it is its significance that determines the response to it. For example, the banging of a door in a strange place does not produce a response in another person unless they attach to the banging a certain significance. They may be expecting a visit from someone, or hoping that someone does not come in upon them. This endowment of a perceived stimulus with emotional 'significance' is 'apperception', which is the process whereby some perceived object has special emotional significance for the individual. A knock on the door is heard and recognised as a door bang, but if the KGB is expected, the noise becomes a 'knock on the door' and is dreaded.

A variation on this theme was provided by Raul Hernandez-Peon's demonstration in the late 1950s of the phenomenon whereby attention to a stimulus in one modality suppresses the response to a stimulus in another.[1] Intractable pain, as it is called, occupies and becomes the centre of attention, and everything else becomes suppressed. The patient with intractable pain cannot function because they can think of nothing else. Other stimuli do not compete and the patient lives with unintegrated, unsuppressed responses to pain. If this is so, the measures conventionally taken to reduce pain – drugs, tractotomy, surgery – may draw attention to this pain and may not succeed because they consolidate pain in its position as the 'centre' of attention. The side effects of many drugs that reduce pain include a dulling and clouding of consciousness so that pain becomes cruder and more diffuse – and the effort and discrimination required to attend to other stimuli, despite pain, becomes more difficult. More drugs are given until not only the sensory input and response is diminished but consciousness to external stimuli is virtually lost. An unpleasant state of dysphoria is induced – not oblivion, but as in a drowsy hypnogogic state. Internal stimuli take precedence over external stimuli. Real oblivion, or refreshing sleep, is impossible – the former because of the inhibition with the flotsam and jetsam of unconscious thinking floating up into consciousness, and the latter because the natural sleep rhythms are disrupted by virtually any heavy analgesic or sedative medication. The refreshing drowsiness associated with a return of the alpha rhythm (seen on the electroencephalogram (EEG) as a 12–15 cycles per second rhythm coming from the back of the brain in all people in a state of drowsiness) cannot occur.

Example of patients with intracranial noise

Patients with tinnitus provide us with an instructive paradigm. It is possible with such patients to reverse the process described above. Attention to other stimuli can suppress responses to the tinnitus. Exhorting the sufferer to become involved and therefore attentive to other things, particularly when the internal noise is at its worse, produces suppression of attention to the inner noise and its intrusiveness is abolished or reduced. In one case the patient was referred because he had attempted suicide. He was almost completely deaf. The patient would speak and describe his dreams and I responded by writing on the pad my interpretations. The sessions proceeded very rapidly and the patient, who dreamed profusely and vividly, was very interested and impressed. The analysis and the interpretations engrossed him and the tinnitus ceased to be a distraction and, in fact, it was never to trouble him again. Another patient similarly treated by psychotherapy came for a follow-up appointment after a year. He was now involved in a successful new business life. When he had come for help originally he had been unable to work for more than a year due to the tinnitus and its effects. Now when he was asked directly if he still had the noise in his ears he said 'Now that you mention it – I become aware of it, and I know it is there but it does not bother me!'

Another supporting piece of evidence for the theory that awareness of pain can be suppressed is derived from a study I made of patients with loud intracranial noises (or 'bruits'). The noises could be heard with a stethoscope and recorded by me, but the patient only became aware of them when their attention was drawn to them. The intracranial bruits were produced by angiomas – abnormally shaped arteries – in the skull. Often patients said that they had become aware of the bruit in childhood and had thought it to be a normal universal phenomenon. One young woman said that she was shocked to learn her 'noise in the head' was abnormal. She discovered this when the angioma produced an epileptic fit for the first time and the angioma was heard by the neurologist. She was a successful professional woman, who had been, to my surprise, unperturbed by the very loud pulsating bruit that was recorded.

In other instances, the noise generator was an extensive vascular malformation that was congenital. An injury or shock then seemed to bring it to the patient's attention and they complained of it as it had arisen since the injury. For example, a young coal miner was knocked unconscious by a fall of rock. He had concussion but there were no fractures. He complained of an intracranial bruit and was adamant that it had not been present before the accident. A loud noise was indeed heard on auscultation and with angiography a network of abnormal blood vessels covering the whole cortex were demonstrated.

This supports the theory that the suppression of stimuli (elimination from consciousness) such as pain or noise is possible if attention is engaged elsewhere, which is an everyday experience. It follows, therefore, that questions during examinations direct attention to the pain and the pain becomes the centre of attention. Attempts at pain relief, which also direct attention to the pain, may also be counterproductive. Attempts to reduce distress from pain should ideally be accompanied by psychological manoeuvres to divert attention away from it. Rehabilitative creative activities and self-exploration in psychotherapy achieve a distraction for the patient and changes are possible even in the most unpromising circumstances.

Receiving the pain of others

Throughout our lives, our view of the world is influenced by the reactions of others. The baby initially experiences the world second hand. Tranquillity or anxiety in the mother signals safety or danger. In some respects, this continues into adult life when in certain situations the adult reverts to being a baby (as in a panic in a crowd or in the presence of a violent lynch mob). Anna Freud observed mothers with their babies during the bombing of London in the 1939–45 war.[2] Despite the loud noise of a nearby bomb explosion and falling masonry, the baby whose mother was calm slept through the disturbance. If the mother was anxious and fearful her baby became fractious and irritable.

In hospital the same influences obtain. The outpatients department brings the newcomer into an atmosphere of anxiety and trepidation and the latent fears and anxieties of doctors and nurses may also signal danger. The quite dramatic change that often occurred at the mere initiation of psychotherapy with cancer patients may have been due to the atmosphere

I created. In representing calm and a philosophical stance with regard to the illness and death, there was no trigger of panic in the patient.

'As good as dead'

Patients referred to me because of intractable pain that had not responded to surgical or medical measures ceased to be preoccupied with it and, as psychotherapy proceeded, diamorphine and other analgesics were discontinued or reduced considerably. This even occured when the diamorphine dosage was being increased for patients thought to be 'terminal'. Despair can be the prelude to death, as the patient perceives the pain signals and the therapeutic impotence as evidence of hopelessness and impending abandonment by others. The fear of disintegration, of going to pieces, arises when an individual feels that he or she is regarded as hopeless, 'as good as dead', by others.

This was described by Walter B. Cannon in his article on 'Voodoo Death', published in 1957.[3] The Aboriginal Witch Doctor would point a bone at his victim, a person doomed to die. After he 'bones' his victim in this way, the rest of the tribe perform a ritual act of burial in front of him, indicating that they have no hope for him now. In their minds, he is already dead, and he is eliminated as a person with any hope. The Aboriginal victim, as a consequence, stops eating and drinking and becomes mute as he waits for death. He stops talking (just like the 'good patient'), and because the others withdraw love and hope, he dies. The Witch Doctor and the tribe see his death as a consequence of the ritual, but it is their withdrawal of compassion that kills him.

Seeing the world through others' eyes

Like a baby, human adults see the world through the eyes of others, particularly those they fear or respect, such as experts. What these others see, rather than what the person sees, affects that person profoundly. For example, a man was apparently calm and integrated as he awaited the results of some blood tests – part of a 'check up'. The next moment he disintegrated, collapsed and was incontinent having been told without preamble that he had a blood disease that could not be treated. On such occasions the patient may be told curtly, with a look that indicates that they alone have the load and no one to share it. The informant seems to look at the patient as if he or she is an alien – outside the normal healthy group. As there is nothing to be done, the quicker they go the better, and the patient often apologises for being a trouble or wasting the doctor's time.

A human being and his or her pain needs to feel accepted with calm confidence. The pain, in effect, can be taken away and something given back with the pain removed – an arm around a shoulder for those we hardly know, and an embrace or a kiss for those with whom we are intimate – as we do with children who have just fallen over! In the physiotherapy department, a senior physiotherapist was explaining treatment to a recently widowed lady and, seeing the pain in the woman's eyes she remembered that her husband had died. She asked, 'When did your husband die?' and then she immediately said 'Come here'. The patient moved towards her and the physiotherapist gently brought her head to her shoulder and hugged her. It only lasted moments and then they moved apart, the physiotherapist continuing to explain the treatment. The patient said that she did not realise until then how much she had missed 'the human touch'.

The complementary approach

Perhaps no procedure aiming to alleviate pain and suffering can be evaluated adequately unless maximum attention has been given to the mental state and the appearance of objects in the 'inner world'. Fear and persecutory feelings may then be converted into feelings and concern for others and *can be borne*. Perhaps all attempts at alleviating pain – mental and physical – should involve a 'complementary' approach. The 'complementary' approach as I term it involves two different perspectives on the patient. There is the medical, physiological perspective and the psychological perspective, which takes in the emotional aspects and the personality and character. The two perspectives are ostensibly incompatible. The medical/physiological perspective cannot be described using the psychological perspective, and vice versa, but both views enhance our overall knowledge of the individual person. The eminent physicist, Neils Bohr, enunciated the principle of complementarity in response to quantum theory in 1958,[4] so-called because light can be described in terms of wave motion or as travelling in quanta, which are small 'packets'. The two perspectives on light adumbrated by Bohr are incompatible in that one cannot be used to describe the other, but taken together they enhance our knowledge of the phenomenon.

Cancer and pain perception

There are certain difficulties in speaking briefly about cancer and pain perception. To communicate with one another we need to be alert to certain conceptions and misconceptions. The word 'cancer' may mean different things to different people of different states of mind, and it can be synonymous with pain or a sentence of death; the mark of a victim, of sacrifice and agony. Almost universal is the belief that one can die of cancer. In fact a person with cancer dies, like anyone else, because the heart stops beating and the supply of blood to the brain ceases. The cancer is not the cause of death but it causes blockages and, by its presence, interferes with the function of systems, which ultimately fail. In the end, death occurs when the heart stops and the brain dies.

In the case of cancer, therefore, although we use the word 'death' more often than not, frequently we are discussing life. When we discuss the experience of having cancer, we are actually considering the trans-formation that can occur as the result of a few words, such as 'Yes, it is cancer', 'It is leukaemia', 'No, we are not succeeding', 'Not very long now', 'Maybe weeks'. Rarely do we ask 'How shall I live until I die?' and rarely is it expressed that we feel scared. In passing it may be noted that the same words used by different people, or met with at different times, have different consequences. The question unspoken is 'Can you bear me and my fragility?' The unspeakable truth, does it bring us together or does it separate us?

The psychotherapeutic approach, as I have mentioned earlier, is alien to most doctors with a scientific training, it being the antithesis of what is taught in physical medicine. The aim of psychotherapy is to enable the patient to suffer, rather than to suffer from the ails of life, whereas the proper aim of the physician seems to be the elimination of pain and disease. Whereas the physician and surgeon, with patterns of disease in mind, look for signs and symptoms of syndromes that categorise patients and their treatment, the psychotherapist conversely tries to empty his or her mind of preconceptions about the effects of the illness or the outcome of their intervention on a particular person. As with pure research, the 'unknown' cannot be anticipated. Instead of planning regimes and treatments that have objectives (like applied research) to which the patient is passive witness, the psychotherapist engages in a dialogue in which he or she is active. Patients, and their relatives, have their view of life transformed by the knowledge that the cancer incubus inhabits their body. Some, in their efforts to restore the status quo, try to ignore the evidence of its spread and act as if they do not know of its presence. They are then indignant and complaining. When it 'progresses' or 'recurs' their indignation and complaints seem justified.

For the psychotherapist there are significant differences between therapy in the presence of cancer or, as it has been called 'an irremediable state of terminal illness', and therapy with patients in other circumstances. Applying the techniques and knowledge derived from psychoanalysis in the milieu of the cancer hospital, the psychotherapist takes time with the patients, and whatever their condition the psychotherapist uses all his or her resources. The amount of time available varies, but it is much less important than the quality of life lived in the time remaining.

In hospitals, the thrust of symptoms and treatment perform the function of denial, which is a vainglorious affair. More often than not attempts at denial take the form of a charade, involving relatives and attendants and it produces an unhappy stasis. The first thing a distressed patient may ask is 'I'm not getting better, am I?' as if a promise had been broken or all their expectations confounded.

The burden of failure

One young man with Hodgkin's disease felt that he could not stand another course of chemotherapy as each of the previous two were thought to be the last. His wife's disappointment at the failure of his treatment was associated with a severe and generalised dermatitis. At home he crucified her by making impossible demands of her while she tried to comply, bearing in mind his precarious physical state. But the worst burden for her had been the discovery from another patient they they could not have children because of the chemotherapy. There had been no warning of this and, consequently, no attempt to preserve semen or even on the part of the couple to try to conceive before the treatment started.

The old fiction that one doctor should and can be in charge of each case and can deal with patients' emotional reactions unaided is dying out, and is impossible in cancer treatment where many specialists are involved simultaneously. Understandably, it is difficult to have to tell any patient, directly, the nature of their illness. Some may even demand its name – the dreaded name 'leukaemia' or 'cancer'. But to have to tell the recently well adolescent of the consequences of treatment is even more painful. And there is the ensuing nausea, malaise, infertility, loss of libido and loss of hair. But when the patient is not told, instead picking it up bit by bit, shock by shock, from other patients and their relatives who see the disease at different stages, it fosters mistrust and despair. Patients need private time and the company of someone prepared to listen and expose themselves to their mental pain. One reason for referral to the psycho-therapist may be a reaction that cannot be coped with, although the treatment may have been 'successful' or the best that can be done.

Knowing all there is to know

After treatment of breast cancer or a brain tumour, the patient may be left disabled, complaining and unpacified. A brain tumour may be removed with little prospect of recurrence but along with the tumour the patient may lose his or her capacity to work and live independently. In my opinion, the decision to operate knowing the consequences requires serious discussion and consideration by many people. The known precedents need to be made clear to the patients and their relatives. The predictions, and the unreliability of predictions, of impaired mental capacity, for example, should be discussed. Sometimes treatment other than complete removal of the brain tumour may be considered, to limit the brain damage and loss of faculties. Having the necessary facilities, organised and focused on caring for the severely damaged patient, is important. I have described instances where the cancer 'cure' – removal of a brain tumour – has also removed the mind in its completeness and produced a peculiarly distressing situation for the families of patients. My involvement was invariably requested after the damage was done, when the situation was irretrievable. The anger on the part of relatives that I mentioned towards the damaged patient, could, with preparation, be avoided. It is not only a person, the patient, that is lost, but the family's relationship to the patient is also damaged. The person they knew has been taken away, and those who took him away have no remedy and no recompense.

'Controlling' pain

The problem of 'controlling pain' is ever present with cancer, and drugs and surgical procedures are attempts to achieve this. Frequently, patients are referred because they complain of pain despite all measures to prevent it. The source may be ascertained or the patient may be thought to be exaggerating. In fact, as I outlined at the beginning of this chapter, there is something mysterious about 'pain', which I think is partly a semantic problem. Pain, unlike an optical, auditory, olfactory or tactile experience cannot be recalled as an image. But we speak as if we can recall it when we really only remember the vehicle or container of the pain, the situation that contained pain. When pain is present it colours and transforms all that is perceived in the past, present and future. A pain-free past may be mourned, but it cannot be imagined, there is no image of painlessness comparable to that imaginary fare of the starving man. Anger on both sides of the fence may be generated when the complaining continues despite everyone's efforts. Doctors are blamed for not paying enough attention to the patient, or there are veiled and explicit accusations that the last manoeuvre involved the 'mistake' which led to the pain getting worse. The pain is complained of as an agent provocateur that destroys and spoils everything. In the course of psychotherapy, as I have already mentioned, pain often ceases to be an issue as if the original complaint had some additional purpose other than to remove pain.

Palliative treatment

Many drugs are given for the relief of pain but quite commonly in my experience it was possible to reduce all the drugs during and after psychotherapy, even 'last-resort' drugs for a time or altogether, with no further complaint of pain. Drugs were a life-belt, and it was as if people saw that life-belt or were pushed into taking it, and took it automtically even though they could swim! Very often a drug will have been given during a trying period and may have been continued because of the patient's fear of returning or worsening pain. I am not speaking, of course, of acute pain but what may be called 'chronic pain', pain that is a constant reminder, presaging something worse. The pain may be 'there' lurking in some site in the body to emerge if a certain move or position is adopted.

Cancer phobia

A patient was referred to me because she had, the note stated, 'a cancer phobia' and was panic stricken because she had been diagnosed as having cancer of the cervix. It was a very low-grade cancer and the prognosis was 'very good'. This meant that the oncologist thought that it would *almost* certainly be eliminated with treatment. The treatment was to be radio-therapy but before it commenced she was distraught and was pessimistic about the outcome. The more the staff reassured her the more cynical she became and did not believe that she was being told the truth. Cancer was the diagnosis and that was, she said, a death sentence and she resented that it had been passed on her. She was so tearful that she was barely able to speak and when she got home she had to tell the eldest of her four children but did not want to tell the others how ill she was. She had been given vague answers to her questions by various doctors and this increased her suspicion that she was not being told the truth and she mistrusted them. What she wanted from the doctors was a definite answer to her questions 'Do I have cancer?' 'Will it kill me?' The truth was that no one could answer these questions as she wished, they could only answer with possibilities and probabilities, and she wanted certainties and she wanted to know what would happen to her, not what happens to the majority or the minority.

When we met after the commencement of radiotherapy, she was distressed, and I think that she felt that she had her worst fears confirmed, because she felt ill and she had diarrhoea. No one had forewarned her that the treatment would make her feel ill and give her diarrhoea. She was hostile and angry because she had felt perfectly well before coming to the hospital. Her peace of mind had been shattered and so had her good health. She was just about to return to teaching and she thought that now this would be impossible.

Her freedom from oppression came with gained insight. She realised that everyone's life is a life lived with doubts and uncertainties. Her search for certainty had led to the painful frightened state that she had found herself in – she was then able not only to have some sympathy for the doctors who could not give her the reassurance that she craved without lying. She was able to assimilate the reality that although nothing was certain she was fortunate. The cancer had been detected before it had spread and it was easily treated. She could tell her children what she had put herself through and how as an object lesson for them she had come out of it to realise her good fortune.

Such patients are so secure in their belief that they are inviolable that they do not consciously consider the possibility that they might have a life-changing disease. Because cancer is equated with death, finding out that one has cancer often causes a complete collapse of belief in anything other than the death sentence. This patient had the fantasy that the doomed victim is never told the truth. With all the reassurances and attempts to comfort her she felt like the victim of the executioner in Nabokov's 'Invitation to a Beheading'.[5] Ironically, she would have lived on as an unhappy woman waiting for death, afraid to tell her children and depriving herself of the return to her professional life.

In the following two cases, there is mental pain and suffering following what might be considered successful treatment. In both cases the cancer was removed, apparently completely.

Coming to terms with successful treatment

A young woman was referred, ostensibly for increasing obesity. This was following removal of a cerebral tumour and then irradiation. The removal was complete and there had been no recurrence but her weight had increased considerably and it was thought that there was a 'psychological' component. In the psychotherapy sessions, she described her mother as overbearing and said that, prior to the operation, she had pushed her to be a beauty queen. She had been successful and had been on the fringes of the film industry. Her mother pressed her to maintain her figure and beautiful presence but, with the increase in her weight, she was violently rejecting her mother. The 'success' was now a failure: she was still under the mother's spell and threatened suicide if she could not lose weight and the isolation and maternal rejection. Before her operation she had been vulnerable and dependent on her mother but with psychotherapy she came to value the life that had been saved by successful cancer treatment.

'Seeing' dirt everywhere – projections

In another situation, successful treatment led to a psychological crisis that also required intensive psychotherapy. A rather elegant man had several operations for cancer of the bowel and had been superior and self-congratulatory after each one until the last operation, which left him with a colostomy. He was 'demolished' he said. Although he was cured of the cancer, because he was obsessive, he was seeing dirt everywhere. He said he could not touch the colostomy and now felt perpetually unclean. He had liked cooking but he now felt that he was too unclean to handle food. We had several sessions, during one of which he asked for an explanation of what had been done to him. When I explained that a mass of tissue that had contained the cancer had been removed he said he felt cleaner because in his words a dirty thing had been taken away.

This man was the eldest of a very large family and had to bring the others up. Clearly he liked this role and he had even cooked for other patients on the ward after criticising the catering. He described an extensive symptomatology in keeping with his obsessionality. He would not let anyone touch him until he had bathed and he described how he could not stand ugliness or abnormality. He was, for example, 'horrified' when he saw a person with Down's syndrome. Under the stress of having a colostomy, he had to engage in psychotherapy otherwise he could not live normally and he could not leave hospital. He did review his life and his attitudes and he developed enough insight to change, and began changing the colostomy himself before he left hospital. He did understand that he saw dirt and faeces everywhere, using 'saw' in the transitive sense – he put it there. He attributed unpleasant things to other people and felt that they looked at him with contempt and pity, which he could not bear. He changed dramatically in the course of several sessions of psychotherapy, a change that would not have occurred had he not had therapy in these circumstances.

In this chapter, we have seen how pain transmits in all kinds of ways. There is physical pain, but there is also mental pain, a suffering as well as a suffering from disease. A psychoanalytic psychotherapist should be equipped by experience and training to investigate and understand the complexity of human experience of pain, and the therapist has to endure to be effective. Whereas the scientist necessarily deals with representation of things, atoms, molecules, cells, we have to be on the *qui vive* for the tendency to treat people in the same way, as 'the case in number 10', 'the big tumour on the right'. Palliative care can only do so much, and sometimes it clouds consciousness to such a degree that the patient is unable to think clearly, or achieve a psychological independence from the trauma of having cancer.

Notes

1   Raul Hernandez-Peon & M. Donoso, *Influences of Attention and Suggestion upon Subcortical Evoked Electrical Activity in the Human Brain*, Proceedings of the First Congress of Neurological Science, London: Pergamon, 1960.

2   Anna Freud and Dorothy T. Burlingham, *Infants without Families*, London: Allen & Unwin, 1944.

3   Walter B. Cannon, 'Voodoo Death', *Psychosomatic Medicine*, 19, 3 (1957), 182–190.

4   Neils Bohr, *Atomic Physics and Human Knowledge*, London: Chapman & Hall, 1958.

5   V. Nabokov, *Invitation to a Beheading*, Trans. Dmitri Nabokov in collaboration with the author, New York: G.P. Putnam's Sons, 1959.

Chapter 6

Dread and trauma – on being told the truth

The moral issue is not simply whether or not to tell cancer patients the truth but that it is more important to know how to do so. Lies and the bald unprepared-for truth can both be damaging. Time and trouble are needed to understand and know the patient and to help him or her understand their situation. Putting oneself into the patient's shoes, as doctors so often do, is the best way of *not knowing* what another feels. Such misunderstanding can lead to medical decisions based on nothing more than fantasies – uninspired guesses about what other people think and feel. It is the equivalent of prescribing for patients without examination.

Telling the truth

The question whether to tell a patient the truth usually arises in connection with cancer. One would expect it to arise with other diseases but it does not do so in the same way. There does not appear to be the same debate about telling patients they have disseminated sclerosis or coronary disease as there is with cancer. The issue, therefore, is not simply a matter of telling the truth, it is a matter of telling the truth in one circumstance and not in another. Thus what the word 'cancer' signifies to the patient is supposed to influence the doctor in his or her decision to lie about the diagnosis. In fact, I believe the decision is more influenced by the doctor's own feelings about cancer than by the patient's. Virtually all patients attending for diagnostic, exploratory, or other procedures, in the early stages of any malignancy, have in mind the possibility of cancer. The doctor's decision, therefore, is not whether to tell the patient the truth, or to deny it, but whether to play out a charade, with the patient, of normal life and prospects, in the presence of incontrovertible symptoms and signs of the 'abscess', 'blockage', with an added diminutive, as in the phrase 'It's just a little growth'. This may mean, for example, a patient knows that his wife knows, but they do not speak of it to each other! The doctor's decision to initiate this restriction on free speech, and the truth, disrupts any normal intercourse so that couples, instead of growing together, wither in each other's arms.

In many diseases the doctor, not necessarily concerned with the truth for its own sake, may press home 'the truth' in order to induce patients to submit to unpleasant procedures that they would (it is presumed) wish to avoid. Less commonly, and with less effect, the truth is used to induce a patient to change from a destructive way of life. For example, an attempt may be made to activate an obese, physically inert individual into constructive adaptations after a heart attack, by telling him he is in grave danger if he does not change. With cancer, however, a point is commonly reached when it is believed that nothing more can be done by the patient or the physician, to alter the course of the disease. This is also the case with, for example, multiple sclerosis, where there is no alteration in life-style that we know of which can materially alter the progression of the disease. However, the patient is generally told the truth, although the manner of dying is anticipated to be more painful and difficult than it is with most forms of cancer. What a patient is told about the diagnosis and outlook may be determined by the fantasies about the illness and reactions to it in *both* physician and patient, rather than by the nature of the illness itself. Physicians may know the actuarial realities of a disease, and its outcome, and they may use these to avoid describing the various real-life scenarios that characterise life with a particular disease. The statistical prognosis may be used to justify optimism, and a particular form of treatment. This is the most pernicious form of lying because the statistical 'odds' do *not* tell people what they really want to know: their personal prognosis. At best this ploy encourages a short-lived gambler's euphoria.

The medical attendants have fantasies about the consequences of telling the truth, and this often determines their behaviour in the presence of patients. The most common 'philosophy' for action is to avoid mentioning the word for as long as possible. The 'worst' often being an eventuality, if the patient and his or her resources are unknown to the doctor, conjured up in fantasy.

Conspiracies of silence

For example, a young woman of 22 came from a hospital, where she had attended but had refused to continue. She had been studying physiotherapy before she got married. After her first baby was born she diagnosed that she had cancer of the clitoris. She told the surgeon this before biopsy and operation. When she arrived on the ward, prior to operation, she so dismayed the ward Sister by telling her the diagnosis, that the Sister asked immediately for an inquiry to find out who was responsible for her knowing the diagnosis. At a later date the patient saw another doctor for radiotherapy and he infuriated her by trying to persuade her that she was mistaken in thinking that she had cancer, and by putting on an act that she thought was an insult to her intelligence and character. She was so hurt and mortified that she refused to re-attend that hospital. Once, during a discussion with me, she said that patients should be told the truth . . . and then she had to stop short and she paused as she absorbed the truth, the truth about herself; *she* actually had cancer. *She* was a patient. Transiently she said that she felt that she was discussing something that happened to other people. She went on to describe how her father had died when she was 12 years old of cancer of the lung. Her mother was told not to let her husband know. Her mother was still distressed and guilty at having obeyed this injunction. She still wondered what her husband had thought and needed. The patient felt that the conspiracy of silence had prevented them from sharing his most intimate thoughts and she still wondered if her father had wanted to say something special to her before he died. This woman was intelligent and sensitive and I was asked to see her because it was thought that, knowing her condition, she would become depressed. She discussed her life without reproach. She was sad without being persecuted or resentful. She could manage her pain, her discomfort, and her relative isolation, without anyone, but she seemed to value the discussions. Although it was a privilege to talk to her, few had the courage to do so and significantly nurses, all her contemporaries, rarely chatted with her, presumably because they were frightened of the challenge she presented, knowing her diagnosis and too readily seeing themselves in her place.

Who decides?

A patient can be given bad news in many different ways – none can make it good! Patients may be told without having to ask questions or they may be told the truth in response to a question. Should people be told that their remaining life is very limited, and the way it will end, even if they do not ask? Alternatively, should they be told to give them the opportunity to discuss their life and its future? The patient may need to make various arrangements and preparations for his or her death. Is it then ethical or fair to decide, with or without the patient's knowledge, what he or she should or should not know about his or her own life? Is it right to assess a personality, and its potential, without knowledge of its strengths and weaknesses, after a brief contact arranged for an entirely different purpose? The position is rather similar to knowing that an individual is going to have to perform a task requiring considerable fortitude and endurance. The individual is kept in ignorance of the true nature of the task on the grounds that it is best not to anticipate an unpleasant experience, so that the individual is shocked and unprepared for what then transpires.

In the telling

The truth can be told in various degrees and there are many variations in the circumstances of the telling. Should people be told the frightening diagnosis bluntly and plainly in five spare minutes in a busy outpatient clinic with no time to give comfort and help them cope with the aftermath or for further questions? Or is it better to tell the patient in conditions of privacy, where time has been allocated and protected in advance (by ordering an embargo on calls and interruptions, for a specific time)? Doctors in general do not know how to pace themselves. In order to generate excitement and an appearance of Herculean labours, they appear nonchalant and are often careless of other people's time. For instance, some outpatient departments are full because a doctor, careless of public dignity, has made fifty appointments at one time. This also has the effect of embarrassing patients into silence and leaving no time for questions.

The truth may be told quite plainly, the diagnosis being given baldly without preliminaries, or questions. On the other hand, a patient may use a pause or take advantage of diffidence in the doctor and ask 'Have I got cancer?' or 'Am I going to die?' The response to these questions may be mature consideration and simply, 'Yes', or 'No'; or 'It would appear to be so', or 'What do you think?' (although this last may appear as a cowardly return of a question unanswered). Despite the doctor's fantasies about what he or she would feel in the circumstances, there can be a presentation of the truth by simple statements, refusing to deny what the patient already knows, and with gentleness, compassion and sensitivity, following the patient's lead as he or she tries to live with the doubts raised by the disease. One patient, for example, not suspecting that anything serious was amiss, went to hospital for 'blood tests'. Subsequently because of the nature of the results, an appointment was made with a physician. Without preamble the consultant presented him with the news that he had a very serious form of leukaemia! The patient collapsed and was incontinent of urine and faeces. One might surmise that had the patient been told by his general practitioner what was being considered, and had he had an opportunity to discuss the various eventualities, he might not have been so defenceless.

A transformation

I was taken by surprise when one middle-aged woman was pushed into the consulting room in a wheelchair. I had not read her case notes or the referral letter. Her husband, who had pushed the chair, disappeared as he closed the door behind her. She was slumped, crumpling in her wheelchair, haggard, grey and emaciated: a woman in her early forties, obviously a shadow of her former self, whimpering with despair. Her first words were, as if surprised and incredulous 'I am not getting any better?' I said, 'It does not appear so'. She said 'I am going to die then?' and I said 'Yes . . .'. She said 'Soon?' I said 'Yes, but I do not know when . . .'. She said 'I want to be here for my grandson's second birthday'. I asked when that would be. She said 'At Christmas time'. That was approximately five months away. I said I did not know whether that would happen. This interview took an hour. During it she visibly altered, she straightened in her wheelchair, and her demeanour changed. She stopped whimpering, and the conversation after these initial exchanges, took quite a different direction. She reviewed her past, and the ways in which she had been fortunate. She had had two sons who had just missed being old enough to have been in the Second World War. The transformation was remarkable, true hope and optimism replaced despair. I asked her why she had in the past seen several psychiatrists. She said that in her younger days she had become depressed at one time, and her general practitioner had referred her to a psychiatrist. As a result she saw eight psychiatrists, but none of them had spoken to her for more than ten minutes at a time, and the treatment had consisted mainly of the prescription of various tranquillisers and antidepressant drugs. She stopped all the drugs and recovered without seeing another psychiatrist.

Subsequently, although her physical condition deteriorated, the patient developed and her relationships with other people blossomed. She succeeded in repairing damaged relationships and resolved a family feud. She had a steady stream of visitors, and was forthright in urging them not to use euphemisms, but to speak plainly about her illness. She told them that she knew what it was, and she knew that shortly she would die. It was interesting to note that one night nurse so enjoyed the patient's company that she often visited her in off-duty time. When medical professionals speculate on whether patients should be told the truth or not, they rarely have this type of experience to draw upon. Their judgement is then based upon fantasy, usually generated by putting themselves 'in the patient's shoes', presuming that they know the patient's mind.

Appearances matter

In another instance I was asked to see a patient because she was due to have a severely mutilating operation in three days' time. I asked for the operation to be postponed, to give the patient time fully to appreciate and discuss the consequences of the operation. She had a carcinoma of the tongue. Its full extent could only be determined at operation and to remove it would involve the sacrifice of all or part of the tongue, and part of the jaw. Subsequently there would be several plastic procedures to remedy, partially, the defects in the skin and bone of the jaw.

Although the patient was informed, she did not understand the options open to her. She believed that the option was either to have the operation or not. The operation she was sure would be successful, the worst would not happen. The possibility of losing the whole of her tongue and with it the ability to speak was described to her, she believed, because the surgeons had to cover themselves by describing the worst that can happen. But, she thought, it never does.

The patient discussed the operation with the surgeon and, separately, with myself. The surgeon thought that the operation was justified because it would make the terminal stages of the disease more bearable: the operation was not to prevent the cancer from extending or spreading but to remove what they could. What the patient was told appeared to be the truth, and she made her decision. But she was not told the whole truth. The patient was told that surgery was an attempt to get rid of the disease and that there was no certainty that it would do so. The whole truth was in fact that whether the patient had the operation or not they knew that she was going to die from the effects of the inevitable extension of the cancer. The various options and eventualities, and the price to be paid in deformity and suffering, for the dubious benefits of the operation were not discussed.

The Sister, an expert in nursing such patients, had no doubts that she herself would not have had the operation. But because the patient was not told the whole truth she said nothing, and she supported a course of action she did not believe was constructive. One can only speculate as to what she would have told the patient before operation had she felt able to. The Sister was in an unpleasant moral position. She disagreed with what was being done and stood by and watched. A bystander, she did nothing to help and after this case she left the hospital and nursing altogether.

In the event, the patient had the operation with partial removal of the tongue and she made great efforts – successfully – to produce speech only to be rejected by her husband on her return home. She believed him to be in love with another woman. In one way he was: he was in love with his wife pre-operation. She had not anticipated the effect on him of her grossly distorted facial appearance and his fear that cancer was contagious. He thought he could catch it by kissing her. After her first operation she was spirited and exultant; she was alive, she could speak and eat, albeit inelegantly, but to her mind the important thing was that she was able to make love and she presumed that this would ensure her husband's desire for her. She had not allowed for the fragility of the sexual impulse in her partner and its dependence on appearances and the intact state of the sexual object.

In my work with mastectomy cases, I have met many times this misunderstanding by the woman patient of the male reaction to disfigurement and scarring of their partner. The extensive scar, the loss of a breast, can horrify someone who has never seen scarring of such an extent.

Postmastectomy depression

A woman was very depressed despite having had a mastectomy from which she made a good recovery. The mental state was so disturbing that I was asked to see her. Depression after mastectomy was commonplace and received no special attention, but in this instance the patient appeared to be more severely disturbed. She had been speaking to all and sundry about her sexual difficulties in great detail as if she was psychologically incontinent.

She was, she said, convinced that her husband was having an affair or many affairs with women and latterly that he was having a homosexual affair at his workplace. She continually checked up on her husband at work and he could do nothing to convince her that she was deluded. Her mental state was thought to be the result of the operation. In fact, both the patient and her husband had separate affairs some years previously and this woman set great store on their sexual relationship being good as proof of their attachment to one another, and of her worth. The husband told me that when he saw his wife's scar he was appalled and he was 'put off' intercourse because he was afraid of hurting her and he felt that she was very fragile. The patient took this to mean that her husband did not like her because of the scar and the loss of the breast. After my first meeting with them, they said that they had a long talk together and that their relationship sexually and otherwise was better than it had been before surgery. Several weeks later the social worker phoned to say that the relationship was still excellent but she added there appeared to be no understanding of what had happened. The psychotic episode appeared to have been forgotten.

Free association

Medical training advocates that the scientific method should be applied in clinical medicine, the aim being to provide conditions that enable observations by one person to be repeated by different observers at another time and place. The doctor looks for signs and symptoms of a disease seen elsewhere at other times by others, so that what has been observed in an experiment to alter the course of the disease can be repeated. Unfortunately, this has encouraged clinicians, who are generally inept and gauche when it comes to observing and studying psychological phenomena, to ignore the whole person to dispense 'psychology' in a few favourite aphorisms, and then to concentrate exclusively on the physical. Generalisations about disease, and particularly about physical signs and symptoms, can be useful, according to this 'scientific' approach, whereas generalisations about personality, character and emotions are generally misleading, although seductive. However, psychological phenomena, although they are far more complicated than physical ones, can be usefully observed and described; this requires different gifts and different methods from those a doctor could be expected to have. The first real attempt to understand and describe mental behaviour was made with the psycho-analytic method. Initially this consisted in listening to patients describing their thoughts freely without questions. The 'technique' was called 'free association', which means the patient is asked to say whatever comes to mind. What followed was understanding of mental processes and the method as a method of enquiry was named 'psychoanalysis'.

The object of enquiry here is the mind and its contents, and physical methods of investigation are appropriate to find out what is going on in the body – but not in the mind. Furthermore, the investigators are *both* the patient and the psychotherapist, partners in the endeavour to obtain a truer picture of what is in the mind. This is not the case with the physician or surgeon. In studying human beings, the scientific method attempts to eliminate the influence of the 'subjective factor'. Psychotherapy, the generic term for derivatives of psychoanalysis, makes the subject – the person – the observer of feelings, also the object of study. The process is difficult, requiring talent, skill, experience and technique, the patient being both an observer and also an unwitting source of distortions of the truth. A patient may seem to be giving an account of his or her feelings, yet, wishing to deny their significance, may play some down and exaggerate others. Obviously the 'observer' will be changed, and the powers of observation reduced by anything that suppresses the brain. Drugs, toxins or alterations of body chemistry that cloud consciousness or produce disinhibition will alter the ability to perceive and the capacity to distinguish between 'inside' and 'outside' in the mind, which is difficult in any event when fantasy (inside) is thought to be 'outside' in the undrugged state. The skill of the physical scientist is evident in the way in which he or she asks questions. Questions are formulated so that an attempt at answering them can be made and the very attempt results in new information being acquired. The main reason for using this method is because it works, but the motive can be anything from the wish to simply discover the truth (pure research) for its own sake, to wanting to make money by finding products that can be sold profitably or to wanting to make more efficient instruments for destroying life (invention and applied research).

Pure research

Psychoanalysis can be likened to pure research (as opposed to applied research, equivalent to symptomatic treatment) and is an attempt to know the truth about what goes on in the mind. Psychotherapy, however, adopts the psychoanalytic technique in searching for the truths that will help people to reduce unnecessary suffering and survive it when it is inevitable. The therapist with conviction based on experience believes that this is the best way of helping individuals cope with unease or disease. From this point of view it would be unethical to help the patient or anyone else to obscure, fudge or distort the truth.[1]

In practice it is both honest, and reassuring, to patients for them to be told that this is the ethic and aim of the procedure, the psychotherapeutic endeavour. Obviously one would not begin to seek out and display the truth without undertaking to remain with patients while they digest and assimilate it: to do otherwise would be like performing a skilful surgical operation and then leaving the skin unsutured, the wound uncovered and the patient deteriorating. For the purposes of treating the disease, the scientist/doctor must know the truth about the physical processes in order to treat and to be able to predict to some extent the course of events. Is it ethical to have this knowledge without letting the patient know what is believed to be going on in his or her body, what risks he or she is taking, and the future that is being planned for him or her? It would be like having a plumber in to examine the central heating system in a house without being told what is wrong, what the plumber intends to do about it, if anything, what the consequences will be for the householder, and above all the cost. It would be intolerable, yet this is sometimes the position of the patient in relation to the medical expert. The patient is deprived of the privilege of knowing, in terms of what he or she can understand, what the expert thinks and prognosticates. The expert then decides the patient's fate without knowing their character and strength – the doctor might *think* that they know, having put themselves in the patient's shoes but, as I have said, that is the best way of *not* knowing what another feels! Psychotherapy, if it succeeds in making the truth available, gives patients the freedom, if they want to use it, to act and to take responsibility for their future.

Doctors' self-perception

Most doctors, if asked about their hospital work, would give quite a sensitive account of the dramas played out in the hospital and in their work. For the most part they would feel that they know how they appear to patients, and would probably have very definite ideas about how they should and do behave towards patients. As Balfour Mount et al. have shown, this is erroneous.[2] Balfour Mount et al. conducted a survey asking doctors how they thought they appeared to nurses and social workers. They asked the nurses and social workers how they thought the doctors appeared. The doctors' perceptions of themselves were quite different from how the nurses and social workers saw them. The study result was chastening and illuminating. The doctors' opinions of themselves influenced their actual behaviour, with obvious miscalculations. For example, a doctor feeling that he was compassionate and appeared so, could be so unreflexive in his self-judgement that he was uncritical of himself; any dissatisfaction he perceived in patients or nurses he regarded as not his concern or responsibility.

Defences against the truth

Doctors rarely consider themselves as victims of the covert, destructive and limiting forces in a hospital. These forces, in the form of social and group pressures, can severely restrict freedom of thought and action. They arise especially when groups of people feel exposed and vulnerable. Living with doubt and uncertainty leads to denial. In war-time this was seen in the humour of the air-raid shelters; the apparent nonchalance of airmen – death-dealing and facing death. Wards for patients with muscular dystrophy – virtually all boys, with none surviving beyond the age of 18 (exceptions reach 20–22 years of age) sometimes have the atmosphere of an air-crew mess. Patients are calm and cheerful, with the weekly news of someone who has not survived the weekend producing a wry comment and barely a ripple in the organised surface of routine and bonhomie. For less constructive purposes, the same denial operates in the staff of other institutions. In psychiatric hospitals in the Soviet Union, which incarcerated dissidents and political opponents of the regime, the staff exonerated themselves from blame by denial. They denied that anything destructive was happening by attributing destructiveness to the victim, or they justified their participation on the grounds that they as individuals were powerless to alter the system by influencing colleagues or superiors by disobeying orders. These arguments and rationalisations have a familiar ring because they are ubiquitous defences against truth and depression. The hospital, where life and death issues condense and concentrate, produces similar reactions in the staff.

Denial

In the presence of pain, imminent death and mourning, there can be amongst staff a cheerful appearance of dealing with the commonplace, as if they have no responsibility for what is happening. Nurses cannot help what doctors do, or fail to do. Doctors cannot act without a superior's permission and superiors feel that they cannot change the system, claiming to be victims of the administration, the political system or inept colleagues. Solzhenitsyn, in *The First Circle*, describes the tremendous effort needed by 'victims' of the Stalinist system to hold on to their independence of mind and retain their integrity under the pressure of torture and propaganda.[3] The forces that coerce and seduce staff are in proportion to the presence of unrelieved stress. Hospital personnel react in a quasi-military style: uniforms, ranks and deferential treatment of staff high in the hierarchical system are how they are ruled. General hospitals manifest such denial, and specialist hospitals, which produce an overwhelming concentration of feared conditions, have even more hidden but rigid ways of preventing the emergence of doubt, fear and independence – like the 'specialist' in *The First Circle* prison of Solzhenitsyn's account.

The hospital produces imperceptible measures to encourage compliance in the patient and the minimum of awkward self-appraisal in the staff. This can be very tortuous. For example, it may become undeniably evident that the large number of patients who have cancer of the breast need something extra by way of consideration of their feelings. The staff, medical and nursing, acknowledge the need, create a post – with a new title, and fill it with a member of the staff. The staff member is no better equipped for the work than anyone was before the new position was created and he or she continues to do what nurses and medical staff should be doing anyway in their traditional roles. The important function of the manoeuvre is to deny that there is a *special* need that none of them are satisfying. This need should be met by a specially trained person, appropriately orientated by vocation and training, being brought in to attend to those areas of care and concern that are being neglected. As far as the new appointment is concerned, the fear is of the unknown; medical staff fear an approach of which they have no knowledge – they react as if issues are going to be raised and forces unleashed that they cannot control. Hence new appointments are given to charismatic controlling figures who can be understood and identified with. In the cancer hospital, as I mention in Chapter 3, the 'military' state of mind is evident in the jargon used: in describing 'aggressive' treatment regimes against 'invasive' or aggressive disease. The word 'cancer' is avoided by referring to 'the disease'.

A 'difficult' patient

This patient was sent to me because she was 'upset' and mistrustful of the doctors. She described how some very painful manoeuvres were performed on her tongue, particularly when implants were inserted and, even more painfully, removed. She had the feeling that she was being accused of faking or acting when she said the pain was excruciating. This was an accurate description judging by the clinical notes. She told me that she had decided not to continue attending this hospital because she was so angry and mistrustful. She described how she had waited two and a half hours for an appointment with the consultant who, when he did see her, was obviously in a great hurry and only gave her a few minutes. In addition, he described her in front of other doctors as 'a difficult patient'. She felt labelled as unusual and unco-operative.

On another occasion, one of the junior staff asked her how she felt about having cancer of the tongue and she noticed that as she described her distress at first learning that she had cancer he was reading a newspaper that had been left on her bed.

In fact, the patient found out that she had cancer indirectly and painfully. On the day her father died she had been to the local hospital for tests for cancer. She had been told that she would be called for another appointment in two to three weeks' time. The next day she had a phone call saying the consultant wanted to see her the following day. She thought that a mistake had been made and they wished to tell her that she did not have cancer after all. At this time she was supporting her mother and was herself grieving over the death of her father. All at once she had to absorb the news that she did have cancer and that an emergency biopsy was required.

In attending to her and her story she gained an insight. She was unusually clear in that she was never afraid of the cancer. She knew that she was expected to be upset about it, but she was never afraid of dying. She now felt that she had something given to her by the hospital and their treatment of her to work through and out of her system. It was pre-eminently the mistrust and anger at not being considered as an individual, as an adult. She wanted to be accepted as a person in her own right (listened to and accompanied as she assimilated and explored these feelings).

This was an instance of the complete misjudgement applied to this patient who was in fact unusually clear and independent in her thinking about cancer and dying. She had been humiliated by being misunderstood and she felt that she had been demeaned because of the incidents described above.

Kafka-esque situations arise because the 'carers' have fantasies about cancer and death and in enacting them may make the unwitting patient suffer. This is a very common situation and patients react to these implicit accusations and delusions about themselves in a variety of different ways. The patients may respond by trying themselves to 'make sense' of incomprehensible behaviour and messages. Some patients are described as 'paranoid' when in fact they are suspicious with good reason. The most common situation is where patients are bewildered. No one has discussed with them the nature of their disease and yet they are subject to various investigations. The most common reason given for failing to discuss the disease and possibilities with the patient is because the investigations are not completed. In fact, the truncated conversations on ward rounds and the vagueness of replies to their questions (to avoid being committed) leaves patients bewildered and suspicious. Even when the news is bad, patients often express relief because the truth removes doubts and gives them a rational explanation for the investigations and for the concern of their doctors. Apart from the painful feeling of being excluded, patients are, by these devices, prevented from considering and influencing their own future. People who are seriously ill for the first time may be worrying about their home, particularly if they live alone. They may wish to plan for the benefit of relatives if the treatment is going to be prolonged. Social workers, if available, may not be able to discuss alternative arrangements because the medical or surgical teams have not committed themselves to a diagnosis and prognosis. The length of time they will be in hospital, the degree of incapacity they can expect and the probable length of time are unknown, undiscussed and imprisoning. This is unethical interference with patients' lives. Their freedom of choice is by these means taken away from them. Thus patients in these circumstances are inadvertently made into prisoners, with others deciding their fate.

The last case illustrates rather painfully some of the consequences of doctors and nursing staff acting upon what is nothing more than fantasies – uninspired guesses – about what other people think and feel. It is equivalent to prescribing for a physical 'condition' to determine if there is one. There is no mental state examination and arrogantly they 'know' the patient's mind without the need for examination.

Uninspired guesses

A 42-year-old man decided, when his cancer of the oesophagus was discovered, to forgo any treatment for it. A year later I was asked to see him because his doctor thought he was 'depressed' but this was not the main reason. The main reason was because an astute doctor realised that this patient was not simply depressed because he had cancer. The patient was an unusually independent man with a dangerous occupation that demanded verve and courage. The patient had been diagnosed a year previously with cancer of the oesophagus but unlike most patients, and those I have already described, he chose not to have treatment.

The doctors he saw did not try to dissuade him but many, without inquiry, had fantasised that he must be anxious and afraid having a cancer, untreated, and certain death imminent. No one had asked him what he thought. The doctor who referred him to me was the first to recognise that this man required more attention and investigation than hitherto.

When interviewed, it turned out he was miserable and puzzled because his vision was blurred and he could not co-ordinate sufficiently to write. He did not know why and he was bored and restricted. No one had explained the drugs. This happens frequently – a succession of doctors without inquiry decides he must be depressed and the 'antidepressants' need increasing or added to by another. None are removed so that patients are frequently found to be having a pot pourri of ineffectual drugs, which depresses them and a vicious circle is established: further medication is given. Doctors have an aversion to stopping medication; by adding drugs or increasing dosage they are less likely to invoke criticism if something goes wrong. Despite the commercial name, all 'antidepressants' are not specific for depression and all have the effect, to a greater or lesser degree, of producing depression!

Some doctors in this situation were afraid of removing any drug. The one who does so then takes responsibility for whatever happens to the patient. If the patient's condition worsens, then prescribing more drugs is 'safer', even if it kills the patient. It is seen as the right thing to do in general, and is what everyone does. It has one advantage, however, and that is that there is no thinking required!

This patient's depression, as it turned out, was due to the side-effects of three drugs, which were 'antidepressants' and 'tranquillisers', and three drugs that were for the relief of pain. I explained why I believed he had been given these drugs. It was presumed that he would be in pain, even though, he said, he had never complained of pain. The tranquillisers were given I presumed because it was thought he would be anxious as death was close. He said that he was not afraid of dying but he was concerned about the possibility of dying through choking with no relief available. In effect he had been given drugs without having a condition that required them, and his ability to think and act as he wished, constructively, had been taken away from him. He had not been told what the drugs were for and they had in effect imprisoned him in a nightmare.

After this discussion, I stopped all drugs and arranged that he went home. He could contact me at any time when he felt he had had enough. He spent the time going over the household affairs with his wife, teaching her how to do many of the odd jobs that he would have done, as he anticipated that on her own she would not, for example, call in an electrician. He taught her how to change a fuse and to understand the electrical mains ring.

Several months later he did phone saying simply that he had 'had enough'. I arranged his re-admission and he was admitted immediately. His oesophagus was virtually closed off. He said that he could just swallow a teaspoon of fluid. He was still a well-nourished, robust looking man and it was as if having completed his task there was nothing more to do. We shook hands and with a significant look – we both knew what we were thinking – we parted. On his third day after admission he died peacefully. He passed away, literally.

The quality of life and what he achieved with his wife was incomparably better than his situation would have been if he had had surgery or any other treatment. At its most successful he may have lived longer, but without speech, without a normal swallowing mechanism. The main reward his wife said was the way that they have lived, loved and worked together and prepared for their parting.

Sometimes the hospital, or part of it, can become like a totalitarian state, with a limitation on the subject's freedom to think and act independently. Perhaps as a legacy of the days of the Poor Law institutions, when medicine was a charity and patients were expected to be deferential and effusively grateful, so sometimes today patients can be treated as if they were privileged to be in the hospital at all and receiving treatment. In fact it is the healthy doctor or nurse who are the privileged parties, as they are by chance healthy and free to be of service to those less fortunate. One feels that what was once urged in retail shops by progressive and enterprising shopkeepers ought also to apply in a hospital: 'The customer is always right!' So, too, the patient is always right, including the patient who complains and the patient who complains too much: indeed the latter may become a patient just because he complains 'too much'.

Meeting a 'patient' is a very special event, a transaction to be handled with great care. The 'patient' in most instances cannot escape the meeting. As the nurse or doctor, one is empowered and able perhaps to impose oneself, awkward and inept, on another. Patients have the power to refuse others entry into their world, but because they hope something good will come of the meeting, and to avoid hurting another's feelings, they hide their misgivings. Staff may thus be misled and, being preserved from self-knowledge by their acquired authority, they shelter beneath their titles and positions, and stalk the wards unaware of the tolerance they are being shown. Often they are manifestly eccentric, assuming as they pontificate, that they are superior to the row upon row of ordinary folk, casualties precipitated into vulnerability. The caring professionals, the healthy ones, may be in great danger, for their personalities, in attempting to cope with this terrible work, can be affected and emotionally blunted in the face of such human suffering.

Notes

1   Power corrupts. Unfortunately, some analysts are so closeted and isolated in their private practice that they can become corrupted and arrogant and cruel in the same way as all-powerful physicians. It is imperative, therefore, that psychoanalytical training be rigorous, open and externally evaluated.
2   B.M. Mount, A. Jones and A. Patterson, 'Death and Dying: Attitudes in a Teaching Hospital', *Urology*, 4, 6 (1974): 741–748.
3   Aleksander I. Solzhenitsyn, *The First Circle* (1949), first English translation by Thomas Whiting, London: Penguin, 1968.

Chapter 7

Psychoanalytic psychotherapy in the NHS 'general' hospital

Up until now, the focus has been exclusively on psychoanalytic psycho-therapy in the treatment of patients with cancer. But a variety of physical conditions also benefit from the same approach. In this chapter, I relate my experience working with patients suffering from other conditions, such as tinnitus and aphonia, and I draw a contrast again between the physical measures taken to remove a symptom and the more indirect psychotherapeutic approach. The patients described here were patients seen in the context of the NHS in Britain, not in the context of fee-paying private practice. Because of this, most of the cases I saw were unlikely ever to have been subjects of psychoanalysis or psychotherapy.

The material for this chapter is based on my experience of practising psychoanalytic psychotherapy in three National Health Service 'general' hospitals. Each of these hospitals was conjoined with an institute specialising in research and postgraduate training: the Royal Marsden Hospital, associated with the Institute of Oncology, the Hammersmith Hospital, site of the Royal Postgraduate Medical School and part of the Institute of Obstetrics and Gynaecology, and the Royal National Ear, Nose and Throat Hospital, a more compact specialist hospital associated with and containing the Institute of Laryngology and Otology.

No-fee psychoanalysis

The practice of psychoanalytic psychotherapy in an NHS general hospital is unusual and special because psychoanalysis as traditionally practised is private and expensive. Each analyst is paid a fee directly by the patient and, in many cases, this fee is paid whether or not the patient attends the session. The session is typically fifty minutes duration and during that time the patient is seen only by the analyst. Whatever the patient says is retained by the analyst in strictest confidence. This practice has always harboured a serious inequity in that only patients with the ability to pay can have psychoanalytic treatment and it excluded NHS patients because one doctor for one patient was deemed impossible. In the work I describe here, the opposite obtained, for there was never any selection of patients based on the ability to pay. The NHS is a unique operation, subscribed to by every working person and affording free medical treatment to all. As an employee of the NHS, I was able to treat patients without payment to me of fees per session.

The Royal National Ear, Nose and Throat Hospital

At the Ear, Nose and Throat Hospital, the majority of patients were referred to me because they had been the subject of investigations that had failed to find the cause of their symptoms. Others had been treated empirically without the relief of symptoms. Others had not responded to treatment based on an apparent, but not real, causal relationship. There were thus a considerable number of cases referred that would be labelled on these grounds alone (failing to respond; no cause found; symptoms unrelated to physical findings) as 'hysterical' or simply 'psychiatric'. These pejorative terms were applied to or inferred without any psychological assessment.

The free use of these terms tells us more about the 'labellers' than the 'labelled'. In fact, these patients do respond very well to short-term dynamic psychotherapy, and those who improve most readily are people with integrated and mature personalities. The fact that the symptoms abate during psychotherapy is merely an affirmation that physical functions are influenced by psychological processes. Further evidence of this comes from the subcategory of cases that improve with psychotherapy but do not respond to physical measures, although they have proven irreversible physical changes. For example, a very common and disturbing symptom is tinnitus (persistent and continuous noise in the ears), which is due to well-described physiological changes. During short periods of psychotherapy, however, tinnitus patients developed new interests, which focused their attention away from the internal noise.

Overcoming the despair of tinnitus

The instance of a middle-aged man who was referred following a suicide attempt because of increasing tinnitus and deafness was described briefly earlier. When he started 'interviews' his deafness was such that verbal communication with him was impossible. He could speak clearly and it was decided to try to communicate by writing to him. The patient slept very little and read avidly everything he could get his hands upon. He had not had a secondary education and he worked with his hands in the clothing trade but he had an excellent memory for everything he had read. He was erudite in psychology, had read widely and could quote from various psychological texts. Fortunately, he dreamed vividly with detailed recall. Interviews became intensely interesting and the evolution of each on the basis of his associations to the manifest content of the dreams was very impressive for him.

He sat on my right in front of a desk. He would tell me his dreams and his thoughts associated with them or features in them. I responded to him entirely by writing. My responses were always delivered as tentative interpretations. Throughout I emphasised that what I proposed or understood was not a certainty or definitive. He was reputed to be irascible and cynical with medical staff but these characteristics were completely absent from our sessions.

Several years later, I saw him again. His spirits were restored and he seemed to be happy, optimistic and fulfilled. He recalled to another doctor how important and favourable the psychotherapeutic experience had been for him, and subsequently he 'referred' his son and separately his wife for counselling and consultation. I am underlining the point that a patient such as this would never had had the experience of psychotherapy had a psychotherapist not been available in the hospital. Also, the resolution of the problem was not affected by the direct assault upon it that 'psychiatry' or 'surgery' indicated, but by the apparently indirect approach of mainly dream analysis in psychotherapy.

In my initial years at this hospital my work as a psychoanalytic psychotherapist with tinnitus sufferers produced a real reduction in the total of such patients attending and re-attending the hospital without relief. Other conditions successfully treated by psychotherapy were functional aphonias, functional deafness and various functional conditions affecting the throat and nasopharynx, all of which generally failed to respond to other measures, including 'suggestion' or the use of placebos. One of the most dramatic but instructive conditions was intractable and exhausting sneezing. In one instance, the sneezing of a 12-year-old girl, which it is impossible to simulate, resulted in several weeks of inpatient investigations, pseudo-rational treatment, without relief.

Family matters

At my first interview with the patient no direct reference to the sneezing was made and the interview was treated as if it were any other introductory assessment of the need for psychotherapy, despite the physical effects of repeated frequent sneezing. It was open-ended, no time sequence or duration was stipulated and I suggested that further interviews would be necessary. I intended to have an interview lasting approximately one hour and make arrangements for more interviews in the future. I did not ask her any direct questions and I did not therefore do the customary review of her history. I merely asked her to say whatever she felt or whatever came into her mind.

Perhaps the way the psychotherapist settles in the chair is a non-verbal communication indicating a willingness to give an hour of life to be used by another. About this person the psychotherapist tries to have no preconceptions, and the person expresses him- or herself and their individual weal. Previously, this patient had been treated not as an individual child but as a disease without the opportunity to express her feelings because no one was interested in them. All discussion and transactions had been centred upon the physical aspects of the sneezing. The cause was guessed at, but there was no evidence upon which to base causal theory.

In the interview the patient described, with obvious pain, her family disintegration. Salient in the description was her fear that her father was going to leave her mother. With an uprush of feeling she described this eventuality and how it distressed her; she felt that it was imminent and she could do nothing about it. She acknowledged that her 'illness' seemed to be effective in holding her father in the home. As he later affirmed, he was strongly attached to his daughter. During the session a transformation occurred. At the outset she was tearful and frightened. This changed and she became profoundly sad, sobbing as she described the family situation and the desolation if her father left them. She appeared to me to be in deep mourning, for the loss of the family as she knew it and for her inability to relate to adults and their feelings. During the session the sneezing stopped. The flow and depth of feeling were so important that I could not help but continue until it came to a natural conclusion and we continued for over an hour and a half.

The patient wet her bed the night after our session. This child was perceptive and I think I enabled a constructive putting together of all her thoughts and the full realisation of her pain with insight. Her fears had not been expressed before and indeed her parents later said that they had not been aware that she knew so much about their difficulties and the impending separation. I had no further sessions with the patient. The family was seen at follow-up and the father decided to stay in the marriage. The sneezing never recurred.

The propitious moment and the quality of the transaction determine the outcome. The quantity of time is not the deciding factor determining progress or the development of insight. In this instance there were the wasted hours as an inpatient, the investigations and the futile treatments, fortunately none of which was damaging.

Other more common conditions can change dramatically with psychotherapy.

Avoiding medical prejudice as to 'causation'

A young woman with aphonia (loss of voice) who had been investigated and then treated with speech therapy to no avail was referred for psychological assessment. She lived with quite an unusual family situation. Her mother and grandmother were very superstitious and with the patient constituted a close trio. The patient benefited in every sense from psychotherapy. She matured, became independent and clear thinking. When the patient was first interviewed there was no voice but she could make herself understood by whispering and mouthing words and psychotherapy was initiated and carried on as it would have been in any other situation. Interviews occurring once a week were offered during which she had to try to say whatever she was thinking or feeling quite freely. This would be an attempt to both explore and help her situation.

It was made clear to her that I had no idea why she had her particular symptom. Therefore the initiation of psychotherapy did not indicate that it was known that there was a relationship between the symptoms and something in her mind. The length of time necessary to have interviews could not, therefore, be assessed. The intention was to help both the patient and myself, the therapist, to explore her thinking in the hope that it would increase her understanding and consequently her freedom to act upon what she observed within herself. This would appear to be quite a normal procedure for initiating short-term psychotherapy but for the patient it was in marked contrast with the limited discussion such a patient could have with other doctors. These would generally be very short, one way, and peppered with direct and indirect accusations of malingering and barely hidden contempt. In initiating a psychotherapeutic process, by contrast, it seemed important to avoid falling into the trap of trying to make direct links between the symptom and the patient's situation. The medical reflex is to search for a 'cause' and make a link between an incident or psychological trauma, for example, and the physical symptom. The 'inquiry' is brief and usually cursory attracting the soubriquet 'hysterical' or, worse, 'malingering'. There might be a psychological 'cause' but a long process of analysis may be needed to discover it; and why if there is a conflict it should be expressed in this way. As I am not questioning or directing the patient with a 'cause' in mind the patient decides what is important.

After two or three interviews the aphonia disappeared and did not reoccur. No direct reference was made to it and the psychotherapy process, using dream material when possible, progressed well. Obviously one could speculate after several interviews and hearing about the family situation that this patient had very strong feelings about her relatives and particularly her husband. A simplistic 'explanation' would be that her aphonia was a way of avoiding the expression of her anger, helping the observer but not the patient with a neat solution.

There are several advantages in practising psychotherapy with the psychoanalytic approach in the milieu of the general hospital. For one thing, all other measures have usually been tried and failed! There are also conditions that appear to be helped by the approach and this can be seen to be the case whereas the improvement in pure neurosis may not be so obvious. Adhering to some of the fundamental principles of psychoanalytic thinking has a considerable advantage over the psychiatric or medical approach. The best instances of this are where the patient has a symptom and, typically, investigations are 'negative'; the patient is then presumed to be malingering or the condition is called 'functional' or 'hysterical'. There are fantasies but no facts about what is in the patient's mind and these are engendered by the frustrating negative investigations. The analyst, it is hoped, would not make such an assumption without evidence. He or she can think of some possibilities but, without evidence, none of them can be acted upon, nor can they be regarded as certainties.

For example, at the Ear, Nose and Throat Hospital I saw five cases of non-stop sneezing. The 12-year-old girl referred to earlier was sneezing every minute during her waking hours and was referred to the psycho-therapist after eight weeks of investigation and attempts at 'treatment', which is time-consuming, painful and costly. This delay in attempting psychotherapy was simply because it was assumed that physical measures could and should have stopped a 'physical' symptom. It is galling to some individuals when the symptom continues despite physical procedures. Accurate, skilled exploration and interpretation in psychotherapy often resolves the problem surprisingly quickly as if it were waiting to be resolved.

The delay in using a psychotherapist when one is available occurred periodically, notably with certain individual doctors who were obsessed with proving a condition was physical and not psychological. In each of the hospitals I attended there were usually one or two senior doctors violently opposed to psychiatry, and even more so to psychoanalysis, as if they were political systems rather than alternative approaches. I used to think that this was because of a fear that psychiatry would take over and usurp their power. The senior surgeon in one place forbade his team from referring patients, but this stopped after he himself became depressed and asked for and received help himself.

These 'conversions' occurred during my term at these hospitals, and they illustrate how ignorant of psychiatry and psychoanalysis some senior doctors could be, and how violently antipathetic they could be too. The dearth of psychological means for helping patients was in part due to this kind of blocking and prejudice by senior physicians.

Hammersmith Hospital: Obstetrics and Gynaecology department

In each of the three NHS hospitals I worked in, patients afflicted with cancer were in different circumstances because of the nature of the functions affected by cancer and the age at which they occurred. In the Obstetrics and Gynaecology department at the Hammersmith Hospital, the tragic consequences of serious illness were accentuated because the patients were frequently young and fertile. Junior staff were bewildered by, although sensitive to, the terrible problems arising in this speciality. Patients were at the beginning of adult life, or at the beginning of marriage, or at the beginning of parenthood. The cancer was usually very rapidly grown and disseminated. In these circumstances there was no consolation from children or a long life lived.

My work in the Obstetrics and Gynaecology department in London highlights the difference between the doctor and the psychoanalytic psychotherapist, and I discuss this more fully in Chapter 5, 'Cancer in different areas of the body and mind'. Many of the problems posed by patients suffering from gynaecological cancer are not considered by the non-analyst in relation to what the individual is thinking.

The example of abortion

To take a common, classic example, if a woman is asking for an abortion the doctor may react to what he or she sees rather than to what the patient sees, by being judgemental. The doctor may consider the woman's situation in society and judge that, because of her age, her intelligence and perhaps her past behaviour, she should be encouraged to have an abortion. The converse may be urged; the doctor may feel that the patient should have the baby and, because he or she judges that the woman's circumstances are good, regards her as irresponsible and to be discouraged. Patients may similarly be dissuaded from having tubal ligation (sterilisation) by telling them that they may lose their children or they may be divorced or widowed and another man may want a child. What the patient has in mind as their view of the world remains undiscovered.

A psychoanalytic psychotherapist, by contrast, wants to know, and wants the patient to know, what is in their own mind. In the process of therapy, he tries to ensure that the patient knows what their decision may involve and its possible consequences. The patient is left in no doubt that, provided the surgeon agrees to perform the operation the responsibility is their own. The gynaecologist, if guided by rigid criteria of his or her own, is in effect taking responsibility for a decision based on what is in their own mind, the product of generalisation and fantasies about other people.

My presence as a psychoanalytic psychotherapist in the department made a difference, and rules of thumb that were prevalent gave way to a more sensitive approach. Both junior and senior staff were prepared to give a lot of thought and time to patients with these problems. In the case of a request for abortion, I wanted to know what the patient had in her mind. Does she have a baby in mind? Some women will say that they are thinking of a child. They have it as a form or shape, even with a name, in their mind. Others say what others have said and it is easy to miss the fact that the patient has not told you what *she* thinks. She may say 'my husband says we cannot afford another child', 'the doctors say I could not cope'.

By trying to find out what the patient feels, one conveys a belief in the freedom of the individual. Liberated from categorisation, the patient often feels an enormous weight lifted. The patient may need supporting but she takes responsibility for the decision. The consultation with the analyst gives the patient freedom to explore possibilities for herself and then to take responsibility for whatever she sets in train. If she decides to have an abortion it is then a request acceded to by the gynaecologist who thinks that that it can be done without danger and without offending, technically or ethically, his or her principles. The patient, for her part, may change her mind next day, her children may all get killed, a new husband might want children, and so on, all of which is irrelevant. Children can never be replaced, nor can husbands or wives. Decisions all through life are of this kind based on present feelings and the hope that, come what may, the future will be accepted without regret.

Another example: sterilisation and sterile discussions

Because the Obstetrics and Gynaecology department had a special interest in the reversal of tubal ligation at that time, many patients were seen who deeply regretted that they had been sterilised at other hospitals. Invariably, this had been done without adequate discussion and without the opportunity to cogitate and appreciate it as their own decision. Commonly, women appeared to have been asked if they want to be sterilised at a surgically convenient time, this could have been just after delivery or at the time of an abortion. These are psychologically the least convenient times for reflection and the making of important decisions. Requests to reverse a sterilisation (or a vasectomy) commonly arise because these procedures have been followed by a complaint of 'loss of libido'. Less frequently it is because of the wish to have a child. In this department there had never been a request for reversal of tubal ligation in patients interviewed as described. This included many young women and childless women. It is interesting to consider the patients who became involved in very extensive investigations and procedures to investigate and improve fertility. Ultimately, they may have become involved in the complex intrusive and very demanding procedures to be followed in attempting *in vitro* fertilisation. The drive for the patient to have a baby of her own becomes obsessive and opportunities, to adopt a child, for example, will be set aside or lost. This has something in common with the feeling of many women requesting an abortion, who found it very distasteful; the prospect of having a baby and parting with it for adoption is something that they could not bear.

Last stories

The following patients illustrate the dilemmas that can be present at the end of life, when they and their family have no one with whom they can confer. The hospital and the nurses and doctors have no room in their work or their minds for non-medical considerations. The cancer explains everything. These patients are representative of many that I saw with a similar pattern and outcome of disease, and doubtless there were many more I did not see. The cancer does not explain the unhappiness of these patients, nor does the fact that they are going soon to die. I cannot underline this too strongly. It is so necessary to discard these universal assumptions and give patients the opportunity to find their way to a resolution of their difficulties and a peaceful leave-taking. Having someone who listened enabled the patients to state their major concerns. My understanding and interpretation of the patient's communications led to the development of insight and relief from anxiety and depression.

The need to be a failure

A 50-year-old married woman was referred because she was observed on the ward to be somewhat garrulous and loudly recanting all her symptoms and speaking continuously about her illness, particularly to the nurses so that all the patients could hear. She had a lymphoma and this admission had been because cancer of the cervix had been newly discovered. She listed a series of misfortunes that had befallen her; they appeared to follow the discovery of the cancer. She felt deserted by her relatives, including her sister and her mother. It was apparent that her situation was not as bad as she averred because she said that her husband was also the victim of misfortune. It was clear that this was not the case and I pointed out that what she told me about herself, her story, meant that she and her husband had been fortunate. The husband and son were not as she alleged they were. In the discussion that developed, the future for her husband and her son appeared not to be as black as she had maintained. In fact, she realised that their well-being and the fact that she had a son was a considerable achievement, she could be satisfied with the things that she had done with her life. She was physically ill; the disease was uncontrollable. She projected her impotence onto her son and husband. This made her miserable, she had done nothing worthwhile and her legacy in her son and husband made them bad and unable to manage without her. The reverse was true and 'reversing' her projections by taking them back, realising that they were her own creations, produced relief and satisfaction. She, like the other patients, was never afraid of death.

Her disposition changed, the pressure that had made it difficult to talk to her subsided and she became calm and cheerful. A month later, she asked to be transferred to a side ward. At this point, she was not taking any form of sedation and periods of sleep alternated with periods when she was quite alert. Her husband stayed with her most of the time she was in the side room and he was with her when she died. The nurse said that she had been washed, changed, and seemed to be very comfortable and peaceful and then having spoken, she merely closed her eyes and stopped breathing.

She had thought that she was leaving behind a very unhappy and unfulfilled son and husband. She worked through this to realise that she and her family had been fortunate and her son would achieve what she wished for him. There was nothing more for her to do and there was no need to complain to get help and pity. She was satisfied with herself and there was peace in her mind.

Overcoming bitterness to care for others

A similar story emerged when I met another patient, a middle-aged woman married to a much older man who was an artist. She had suffered very badly for twenty years with rheumatoid arthritis but, during a seven-year remission, she conceived and had a son. She managed their finances and the irregular income from his work. The son was at boarding school and her deep concern was that her husband being, according to her, careless and inept with managing their affairs, would jeopardise their savings and would not look after their son adequately.

She had been found to have a form of cancer in her groin and another form that was generalised. A request came with the information that she was deteriorating rapidly. She was very angry with her consultant, having asked him to give something for her depression he prescribed a drug that she said dried up her saliva and made it impossible for her to eat.

Because of her husband's ineptness she had invested and made provision for her son to remain at boarding school. She had many plans for her son's future but, in discussion, she accepted that he was going to be well cared for even if her husband died. She was resentful she said because she had been the one in her family who helped others and yet she was the one who was going to die. She was not afraid of dying and without giving a reason she was not eating, although she dressed to cover up her thinness. She used make up and appeared to be trying to present herself as a grand person. Beneath was a deep sense of bitterness and injustice and I believe that she wanted to die by not eating as a punishment for all those in her family who did not care for her as she had done for them. When I first met her she had so much to say, urgently to get it all in, making it difficult to say anything in response. On the second occasion, she was calmer and it was possible to interpose that, as with the patient previously described, she had achieved a great deal and she had arranged her affairs so that her son could continue in boarding school without needing help from his father. I felt that there was a lot more work for us to do but she was too ill by this time. Nevertheless a change did occur, which was, I think, due to the opportunity she had to state her case; as I have described in other instances, a divestment of her grievances and anger. Her relatives were not really to be envied, on the contrary they might well feel humbled by her ability to care for others.

Changing behaviour – changing the internal world

At the patient's request I saw a woman who had twelve months previously discovered that she had cancer of the breast. Unbeknown to her it had been present for some time and had developed rapidly. She had a laparotomy to remove her ovaries. She had asked if there was psychiatric help in the hospital. She spontaneously volunteered the information that she might not leave hospital and she described the shock when she discovered that she had cancer. She was shocked, she said, because she had been so strong in the past, as if she had regarded the development of cancer as something that did not happen to 'strong' people. Her problem was that she had an alcoholic husband and they had two daughters a year apart in age. Her husband could be unkind and violent, particularly when he was drinking. She said that he disliked their eldest daughter and she thought that he could be violent and unkind to her without her protection. I gathered that he had always been unkind to her but, since her surgeon had spoken to him, he had changed. She presumed that the surgeon had told him how serious her condition was. It did indicate that her husband was amenable to advice and had changed his behaviour towards his wife.

This patient was not afraid of dying and she could speak of herself being in the past so strong, vigorous and fully occupied with living without regret.

However, she had a serious problem that she wanted help with in the present.

Resisting disintegration

A woman was referred because she was in a distressed state and because she had herself asked if she could see a psychiatrist. She was described as being 'very disturbed and frantic, knowing that she is in a poor condition'. I came to see her and her husband. She confronted me saying under great pressure; 'I know that I am dying and must face it . . .'. Her tears and words came in a flood – 'I talked it over with my husband and I know there's no hope', but, she pleaded, 'I keep crying and can't help it'. It was as if she had read a book about 'how to die well' and was surprised to find that despite it she still felt afraid and upset. In the first interview it was pointed out that she was using the future tense but in realising that she was in the present, and in her mind, already dying. She spoke of her children and how they would be bereft – she wanted to know how to deal with them. The youngest had not asked questions and the older one seemed to avoid discussion. I said that I could not think of her as someone who was dying as she was alive, vital and living. She was already mourning the loss of life. I suggested that she could live as she might always have lived . . . from moment to moment. I did not agree with her when she treated herself as already dead with no future. If she was very ill, or the attacks on her body were not being held, then that was all the more reason for enjoying every minute of life as it is.

She had known that she had cancer of the breast three years previously and now it had returned and disseminated throughout her lungs. At the beginning of the interview she had difficulty in breathing and talking at the same time, but by the end she was breathing quite comfortably. In a rush she gave all the reasons why she did not want to die: The children, what would happen to them, could they cope? Would her husband be able to manage? She had so much to do and knew that there was very little time. She said that she had been terrified of choking in the night when she was at home and had difficulty in breathing. The first interview ended surprisingly with the patient saying that she wanted to see me again but after a delay, as we had covered so much that she wanted time to absorb what they had discussed. A week later she requested an interview. She then described what had happened in the interim. She and her husband had a week and a weekend in which they had talked and been with one another constantly and she said it had been the best time of their lives. She had lived from moment to moment, with every moment precious. Their lives had now had an intimacy and reached depths that they had never experienced before. She was now able to sleep much of the time at home, even though she knew that the last course of chemotherapy had failed. Another interview was possible but she cancelled it with a note in which she said that she felt so unwell that she did not think it would be any use having an interview. Moments in this woman's life were now so precious, pregnant with new experiences and feelings. They, the feelings, the patient and her husband needed space and time to be protected from the mundane and intrusive routines of the hospital.

When I first met the patient she was disintegrating, but over the course of our sessions together she changed to become an integrated individual who took charge of her life. She decided, in effect, when her life was at an end and this moment was when she felt that she had done all she could to organise her husband and family to cope with her death and absence. Her husband was seen a year later for a brief period of psychotherapy when he became depressed. The intensity and suddenness of the return of his pain at the loss of his wife took him by surprise. A bereavement was worked through and a considerable time later there was a return of the pain and a deep sense of loss was renewed.

These cases illustrate the mental pain associated with disempowerment near the end of life. Even old longstanding difficulties become urgently in need of attention and the patient may feel trapped in hospital with no one to talk to about them. Obviously there are those who cannot initially see the point of talking when it seems to have nothing to offer by way of pain relief or physical cure. In any event, most patients have no experience or knowledge of psychotherapy or psychoanalysis. In giving psycho-analytic psychotherapy in a hospital, the number of interviews is not necessarily related to the outcome. There is an impressive pacing by the patient so that understanding is acquired rapidly once a worthwhile and interesting exchange occurs. Sometimes what is accomplished in months is at other times completed in days; the speed of the process is often related to the physical urgency of the situation. The most important issues are considered and no time is wasted on subterfuge and alternatives. Sometimes death seems to be delayed while the patient inexplicably survives devastating treatment until some work is completed. When integration is achieved, the reality of death ceases to be as important as the fantasy first made it appear and the end may even be anticipated with relief. In many cases, the naivety of patients with regard to psychological treatment and mental processes is an advantage; instead of prejudice and suspicion about the process, there is an exploratory interest compounded by the urgency of the situation.

Caring until the end

One young woman asked to see a psychologist or psychiatrist because she wanted advice. Her husband wanted her to take LSD because he thought the mental stresses induced by drugs would release her and also she could prevent the cancer from growing by mental forces. This meeting led to psychotherapy that continued over several months. Her husband was a devoted and conscientious supporter of the patient and her treatment. The last time she was seen was at her own request. She was a little frightened and asked if I could return the following day, a Sunday, but she changed her mind and said that she could manage. It was the weekend and she did not want to trouble me! She said goodbye to the therapist, and the following day she died. All the interviews were against the background of an inexorable physical decline. Before she finished she had dealt with her very difficult past and the many painful features of her adult life. She had looked after her sad parents, both of whom had cancer, and amended and repaired their relationship to her. Finally, she looked after her therapist, calling me in on Saturday morning but telling me not to come the next day, as she did not want to spoil my Sunday! Reparations, and these acts of love, were the crowning achievement of her life.

Psychoanalytic psychotherapy has more impact and value in helping people who are chronically or seriously ill than in any other field. Because of the seriousness of the patient's life situation, psychotherapy proceeds right to the depths of the psyche without the pretentiousness, the inhibitions and the unconscious manoeuvring that characterise and prolong psychotherapy with physically well patients. The time factor is important and both parties are impelled in physical illness to proceed without delay, whereas with physically well people both parties feel they have a choice and can choose the frequency of interviews and the duration of the procedure. Psychotherapy with physically well people has this as one of its artificialities in that it proceeds on the assumption that there is plenty of time and that life will not be shortened unexpectedly, so that the psychotherapist's procedure can be viewed as having a beginning, a middle, and an end, whereas with the physically ill, the best that can be done has to be done with despatch and it finds its own beginning and an ending unplanned. The physically ill person has a lot of time available because they are frequently not working and are not involved in time-consuming occupations, which make meetings difficult. The physically ill are able to provide the time for interviews and the time to cogitate and assimilate them. The fact that there can be no illusions when somebody is chronically or terminally ill immediately eliminates many of the preoccupations and a lot of the agonising associated with normal psycho-therapy; and career, economic and sexual-erotic considerations may be eliminated from the discussion. The very core of being is available for consideration and matters of protocol are of no consequence. If the comments made by therapists are valid and the interpretations are illuminating and confirmed by the patient's experience the work proceeds without flattery or mutual idealisation. The physically ill patients are very co-operative and whereas physically normal people commencing psycho-therapy might take a lot of time to understand the worth and significance of using dreams in psychotherapy, the physically ill patient understands and realises almost immediately their potential for illumination.

There is an unconscious prejudice against the sick, particularly those who do not get better. They horrify us because we cannot stand the idea that we too can become dependent and incurable. Hopefully there will be an increasing number of people willing and able to train to do psychoanalytic psychotherapy with a view to applying it in this field. The following chapter examines group processes in hospital and discusses ways in which medical staff might be trained to deal with the effect of cancer, and serious illness in general, on the mind. By training staff in this way we may lift sick people out of the emotional slums and despite their weakness, loss of right, lack of value to society – restore them to dignity, integration and self-respect.

Chapter 8

Examining group processes in hospital

Throughout this book I have referred to the importance of good communication between consultants, doctors, nurses and patients within the hospital context. This is the essence, I suggest, of the 'good cancer care' alluded to by the Calman–Hine Report of 1995. In this last chapter, by way of conclusion, I focus on the various forms of communication in a general hospital, emphasising the way in which explicit, implicit and non-verbal forms of communication affect the relationships that exist between various professional groups in hospital, particularly between doctors. These modes of communication are unwittingly designed to pass on information to others while at the same time excluding others who are not in the group. This use of communication to include as well as exclude will be discussed in so far as it affects the transmission of the truth between professionals; the way in which it affects the freedom of the individual; and the corrupting effect that it can have on the character of the professional by reducing sensitivity and compassion.

Groups and gangs in the medical team

Traditional medical training inculcates and encourages a gang-like, competitive group formation. This leads to an increase rather than a decrease in suffering, with a deterioration in the medical professionals' ability to cope with and endure the battlefield-type experience that is involved in dealing with cancer, the disorganization it produces and the painful and very difficult treatments it involves.

The importance, therefore, of proper training of medical staff involved with cancer patients is vital. For most professionals, this training involves 'de-skilling', that is, unlearning for the most part much of what they have been taught. In training doctors and nurses to approach cancer patients with care, the emphasis is on *listening* rather than telling, instructing or directing. The approach to training staff that I envisage and recommend is not via courses or programmes taught away from the place of work, but rather *in situ* training, in the hospital or cancer unit, which facilitates the right kind of care for patients while at the same time providing supervision and teaching for members of the staff, particularly nurses.

Groups and gangs

The interdisciplinary treatment of cancer that I have advocated throughout this book reveals the different ways in which individuals can work with one another. There is the apparent, but not real, co-operation when the group really has the character and nature of a 'gang'. The relationships in a gang are of a political nature because the individuals dissemble friendship and collude with one another to preserve themselves or to gain ascendancy over their companions. The other form of group is rarer and is concerned with an appreciation of the truth. Each individual is more selfless and more concerned with the care of others than with the self.

Use of jargon

Communication can be used to pass information from one group to another, but it is also used to exclude other groups and individuals, and this can be done by the use of jargon. This was the thesis of George Steiner in *After Babel* (1975), in which he discussed the reasons for the proliferation of different languages and concluded that the group or family developed their own language so that they are understood by other members of the group; but at the same time they exclude other groups and members of other families. We know that this certainly occurs when doctors and other professionals are talking among themselves and unwittingly wish to maintain a separation between the medical professional and the patient, but it also plays a crucial part in maintaining and effecting a separation between different groups towards, for example, different specialists and between different professional groups, such as nurses, physiotherapists and occupational therapists. As will be indicated later, this is a very important source of acrimony and lack of co-operation between groups, and its replacement by rivalry and competition, which is to the great detriment of the patient. In passing, one might say that whenever jargon begins to proliferate in hospital there is a proportional increase in danger for the people using it and for the people that they are caring for. The use of jargon can produce cynicism and the purveyors of jargon diminish the individuality of those who are given 'labels'. They themselves are corrupted and feel superior to those they label.

Euphemisms galore

The wife of a young couple asked me one day, with a mischievous look at one another, if she had cancer; I laughed with them; it was so preposterous. She thought she had cancer of the lower spine (in fact she had a rare tumour of the sacrum which produced a noise when she moved; no one knew then whether it was malignant or not, and she did not know if she was doing damage to the sacrum if she moved). The word 'cancer' had been used freely in all our discussions and we had discussed many aspects of it and the effect that it was having on their lives. I asked why she had asked the mischievous question. They then said they had counted up all the different terms that had been used by doctors in place of the word 'cancer'; the list was extensive. One might ask why this word had to be replaced in the various discussions between this patient and her doctors. Ostensibly and in other circumstances it might be said that the word 'cancer' is avoided to protect the patient, but that could not be the case here. She and her husband used the word freely so in this instance one surmises that it was not to protect the patient, but to protect the doctor who had put himself in their shoes and wanted to avoid a discussion of the dreaded topic.

We can, therefore, distinguish between two groups of medical professionals in hospitals. The devices used by the group that uses language to foster a feeling of security in themselves, and to effect a separation between themselves and patients and other groups, include the use of jargon and euphemisms. By 'jargon' I mean words used by a particular group so that it becomes the 'language' of that group. The euphemisms for loaded and frightening terms contain a presumption. The presumption communicated is that the patients will be more frightened and distressed by the use of plain words than by the use of euphemisms. This is a rationalisation and an attempt to justify the manoeuvre. The real reason for the use of euphemisms is to protect the user.

In the case notes on a ward called the 'terminal ward', there used to be a sheet that told the nurse what the patient had been told by the surgeon or physician. The nurse was supposed to go along with the story and with the pretence. As one nurse said to me at the time, 'try telling a young man whom you bathe every day in potassium permanganate solution that there is nothing wrong – when the "nothing" is agonising and his body is increasingly covered with malignant melanomata that look like weeping anuses!' When I saw a physician visit this ward he was followed by a woman saying 'But I'm getting worse doctor!' – he kept on walking saying briskly 'Don't worry my dear – just rheumatism – it'll get better!' I do not need to elaborate upon the message he communicated to his companions, the nurses, the physiotherapist and the greater audience of patients.

Ultimately, this group can be termed 'self-centred' because it is for the protection of its own members. As it is a group of medical professionals, one might wonder what such a group intends to protect itself from: the other groups? patients? This kind of group I call a 'gang', because to a greater or lesser degree it has all the hallmarks of an adolescent gang. In the long run it is destructive, with the prime interest in maintaining itself, and this runs counter to the main function of the hospital, which is to be full of care and concern *for others*.

Co-operative groups

I would distinguish the 'gang' from another type of group, which I call a 'co-operative' group. The aim of such a group is the preservation and care of others without counting the cost for the individuals in the group. The group is united by its willingness to suffer and sacrifice for others with no regard for considerations of group, class or status. As the aim of communication in the co-operative group is to pass on information that may be helpful and constructive, there are no limitations and restrictions on the terms and language used. Whenever language is used, the intention is the same and if any communication is unclear then efforts will be made to clarify and improve the quality of the intercourse. Improved communications are the result. Isolating verbal screens are removed and there is increased freedom of speech between different professional practitioners.

Good or bad care

One nurse said, when describing renal dialysis and the needs of such patients, that the kind of care that she was describing could not be given by doctors, only nurses could do it! When pressed she said that she did not think that doctors would understand! That communication tells us quite a lot about that nurse's view of doctors. Doctors might respond by saying that they give a different type of care with their medicine and surgery. In fact, both sides are committing the same error in thinking that there is a special form of care, be it 'psychological' care or 'medical' care.

This proliferation of different groups, counsellors and specialist nurses, arises from the failure to realise that there is only one sort of care and it is either good or bad. I think this also applies to terms such as 'terminal care' as if there is a special care for people who are 'terminal' when in truth we are 'terminal' from birth. There is essentially only good or bad care. It is not the monopoly of any particular group, place or religion – although the rhetoric and propaganda of some groups try to indicate that it is.

Seeing things from others' points of view

One of the difficulties of communication between different groups, for example between nurses and doctors, is that they see the patient from different points of view, or, more accurately, from different worlds and the need for translating from one to the other is not realised. The nurse who bathes the young woman of her own age, sees her on bedpans, stays with her to commiserate after the brief round and the devastating cursory few words that took away illusions and hope with the diagnosis, enters into and becomes part of the patient's world. The problem is how to reduce in this instance separation between doctors and nurses so that the former appreciate the other view point and can allow themselves to know more intimately the suffering of the staff/patient world (they are inter-changeable) and still continue to be useful to them. This may seem obvious but doctors and nurses and other medical professionals who have been ill themselves know that prior to their own, or a relative's, illness they had not by any means fully appreciated the impact of disease, hospitalisation and treatment on banal, ordinary, everyday life.

How are we to change this and to improve the communication between those who really do know and those who think they know? How are we to recognise when sensitive and compassionate medical professionals need a break? In intensive work with cancer patients, it is imperative that doctors and nurses are able to rest adequately and return to their private worlds where there is no sickness. This cannot be contrived and, contrary to what has been thought, it cannot be produced by the formal discipline or rule book of a quasi-military organisation; people just cannot switch themselves on and off. The problem is, therefore, how do we produce a doctor or a medical professional who is capable of alternating between the sick patients' world and the 'healthy' world without having consciously and deliberately to act; and instead care for and about them, 'naturally' as their own kith and kin.

A training in insensitivity

The training of medical students, while not including adequate training in interviewing and observing patients, does include a training in insensitivity. Medical undergraduate training is generally by clinicians and scientists who are not only without training in teaching (a problem that has resulted in the setting-up of special groups for the study of ways of improving university teaching) but are, themselves, the victims of traditional medical teaching. Most, but not all, continue to use jargon and a medical history-taking procedure that eliminates from consideration the sensitive suffering individual human being. The secret language, jargon-laced with euphemisms, between superiors pitying the poor (inferior) patient makes true intercourse between equals impossible.

In medicine, individuals become 'patients', 'cases', 'the tumour on the left, second bed down', 'the terminal patient', 'the geriatric problem', thus avoiding the pain and the need to consider the unease of the whole person and his or her family that results from a devastating shock, similar to an unexpected explosion, which is caused by the news of the disease and its treatment. The study of physical disorder trains the student in the classification of symptoms and signs of the patterns of disease, thus bringing the patient under the dissecting method, designed to isolate the disease process. As in qualitative chemical analysis, the procedure is to break down the whole into its parts to identify the elements of a compound.

Following the truth

To improve the communication between professionals in hospital regarding their charges one has to consider the meetings with patients, in any circumstances, as a privilege and an opportunity for a kind of research. I am reminded of this because of my training as a doctor doing surgery and medicine, which I now contrast with my work as a psycho-analytic psychotherapist – I see patients in quite a different way. I may see, over several hours, a different patient each hour and I am making the change from one patient to another having listened carefully and responded with great deliberation to each individual. One tries, and for the most part, manages, to stop an interview and with equal sincerity and application change to accept the world of another patient. This change is not consciously made; I do not say to myself I must switch off one mood and switch on to another mood. I think this change can occur because one is doing research with each patient; following very carefully the patient and their thinking, like a research worker, not leading, but following the truth wherever and whatever it may indicate. This is in contradistinction to a medical consultation, in which a patient follows what is advised or described. As a doctor, I already have a pattern of disease in my mind, which I apply, and as a doctor, I am not open to receive freely and without preconditions what the patient has to express. My interview will be quite restricted by the questions I ask; my task is to discover the disease and what causes it.

By contrast, having decided that one is to sit with another person for approximately an hour you communicate to the other person non-verbally, by the way you settle and listen, your willingness to give them the time of your life, whatever their condition. Obviously the response to this offering is quite different from how they may respond during 'normal' consultations in outpatients or on the ward.

Referring back to the couple that I mentioned earlier who had made a list of alternative words for 'cancer'; when I first met them the patient was agonised by pain, which was increased by any movement; when I sat down with her and her husband in this fashion, very tentatively but with increasing openness, they told me that they had only recently got married but they were terrified of having intercourse for fear of breaking bones in the part of the spine involved. She said they had not discussed this with the consultant or his medical team, and she laughed and said how could they possibly bring it up on a ward round, which was her only contact with the consultant, when it lasted no more than three minutes at her bedside. It was a public affair with the consultant's retinue around the bedside looking down at her as a specimen to be studied. Without words, this expresses for the benefit of doctors, the nursing staff and other professionals that happen to be present, what the 'chief' thinks is important and the relative value of his or her time compared to that of the patient. It also conveys the consultant's feelings about the value of privacy for patients and the relative value of his or her time compared to theirs.

The importance of not forgetting

Memories of patients in the two contexts, medical as opposed to analytical, are quite different. Memories of people who have been seen in psychotherapy are rich and distinctive and do not depart, being akin to the memories that we are all aware of after very vivid and moving experiences of exceptional people. The recall is effortless, whereas the recall of other experiences, such as routine physical examinations and the exchanges that occur in the normal medical outpatient routine, requires effort. This is the reason for some of the difficulties in communication between professionals. Many medical auxiliaries have dramatic and outstanding experiences with patients that they cannot forget, whereas many of their doctor colleagues have more superficial experiences, which we know to our cost they can very easily forget. Hence one is often aware of an undercurrent of ill-will and acrimony separating different medical professionals in hospitals, and also between different levels in a particular department. The formation of 'gangs' results in professionals being unable to speak openly to one another, having forgotten that their main concern is the patient. All too easily, matters of protocol and face-saving manoeuvres can override consideration for the patient.

Other important difficulties arise because of the lack of communication between professionals who feel themselves to be at different levels. One of the reasons for this is that although there are no explicit regulations have to be followed, there is in effect a military-type organisation, with ranks related to responsibility. In military-type organisations and situations, for instance, the captain of a ship or the pilot of an aircraft appears to have total responsibility for the crew, but it is to be noted that the crew absolve themselves from responsibility; indeed they may encourage whomsoever appears to be strong and willing to accept responsibility. Obviously, the communication that occurs between captains is going to be different from that which occurs between those who feel that they are without executive power. The latter may suggest, criticise and comment very carefully but may take no responsibility for what transpires.

Slavish compliance

A medical registrar was reprimanded because his letter of referral stated that although the patient had cancer and was in excruciating pain, morphia, which relieved the pain, had been stopped because it was believed that the patient might become addicted. Apart from this being fallacious, the question of addiction, even if it occurred, was not important in these circumstances. At a later date when he had left the hospital for another appointment, he made a special effort to contact me to tell me that, although he entirely agreed with the criticism, his 'chief' at that time was convinced that morphia was addictive and he, therefore, had no option but to comply. It was perhaps courageous to admit this but erroneous to think that he had no alternative; it seemed brave but he was driven by guilt and by what he saw as the necessity of preserving his career prospects rather than the patient's welfare. It became obvious in the ensuing discussion that if it had been his father, son, or brother he would have exercised that option. He could have risked a poor reference or the loss of his job and he could have made a decision to attend to the patient's needs as he saw them.

The 'as if' scenario

To have one set of rules for relatives and self and another for patients is immoral. This form of communication might be called an 'as if' communication. Over and over again one hears in hospital these 'as if' communications by all levels of staff following a lapse or lack of care; it is aimed to absolve the speaker from guilt and responsibility. Knowing the truth yet speaking 'as if' everyone agrees they had no option. The plea that there is no alternative but to follow instructions is inadmissible in any context. Psychiatric hospitals during the communist era in Russia, and NHS hospitals are no different in this respect. We need to be reminded that we have the means by which we can communicate either verbally or non-verbally in hospital and show our respect for patients and their difficulties. There are non-verbal ways of communicating this; quite simply this might be done by the meticulousness with which appointments are kept; by the confidentiality exercised in transactions about patients. When we make it possible for patients to speak privately and frankly we indicate to those outside the room how much we respect the freedom of the individual even if they are ill and have limited power in the healthy world.

Training

To instruct students of all kinds, beginners in psychotherapy, we require a different kind of teaching from traditional didactic methods. *Pari passu* with the 'rational', physical, clinical, medical approach there needs to be instruction of a different kind on the same lines as used for psychotherapy training. Students would have to conduct interviews and subsequently relate them in detail with their own feelings to an experienced senior colleague. This form of supervision would be private, individual and critical. The individual would then feel that he or she is the instrument, here being scrutinised. There would in addition be presentations of individual transactions to small groups of students, with an experienced psychotherapist as supervisor. This may introduce difficulties, as some students, who do not want to be clinicians talking to patients, might find the exposure difficult. But it would at least ensure that individuals who are very unlikely to be capable of interviewing patients would be exposed and forewarned. Some may eliminate themselves from the course, others may never interview but still have a knowledge of the problems, which enables them to support and foster the work of those that do 'interview' and work by psychological means. Arranging to give private, intimate, uninterrupted time to another regardless of their state or position relative to others in any environment requires effort to make it administratively possible, but in a hospital it is particularly difficult. It also requires a lot of conviction about the previous worth of human life as there are seductively easy ways of avoiding the issue and of giving to another a small part of one's life.

The complementary approach

Instead of propounding neat theories about people, encapsulated in aphorisms and generalisations, one would aim to encourage students to free themselves from prejudice and to think dynamically and flexibly alternating between both modes. It is not necessary to reject one in order to think of the other. Instead, a complementary approach might be adopted. As I mentioned in an earlier chapter, in physics, the viewpoint of the observer alters the phenomena observed. Quanta and wave motion theories of light are complementary but different and incompatible – but the phenomena can be observed from either viewpoint without being contradictory. Similarly, human beings can be observed from either the viewpoint of the scientist attempting to understand objective phenomena or from that of the psychoanalyst or sociologist, philosopher, psychologist, attempting to understand the mind.

Encouraging the 'student' however 'senior' to make him- or herself available for experiences from which he or she can learn is the essence of teaching. The teaching must involve discussion of interviews with patients, along with the interviewer's own reactions and subjective experiences. Under the guidance of a senior, experienced psychotherapist this can produce real and constructive changes in attitude. This would be in contrast to remembering facts without feelings. Students would find that their position with regard to suffering could change and they would then feel that they could allow themselves to think about 'the hopeless case'. Traditional medical teaching includes protective devices against emotionality; these include the use of jargon, the short time (if any) given to free and private discussions with patients and the lack of facilities for private discussion. The short time given to the patient/doctor contact can be filled with questions and directions aimed at blocking awkward evocative responses by the patient. Physicians vary and a good physician may consciously choose to stay with the physical disease and its symptoms and leave others to consider, for example, the non-physical aspects of life, such as reactions to unrelieved pain; reactions to the anticipated manner of death; and reactions to the family, social and emotional dilemmas precipitated by the disease and its treatment. Nevertheless, having had some undergraduate or postgraduate experience of psychotherapy the physician would know enough about what his or her psychotherapist colleagues attempt to do, and be able to facilitate and support their efforts.

A good death

Life-draining cancer treatment absorbs the patient and medical attendant alike. It is the beginning of an often short, dark and boring tunnel. The woman who exclaimed, 'I know I'm dying! I've read all the books – and I'm still afraid!' was saying, in effect 'What do I do now?!' She discussed the next permutation of chemotherapy with her surgeon but he told her that it was not working. She asked him when she would die but he replied that there was still time and that she should not be so hasty. But in this case there was nothing else to talk about, they had nothing in common. The disease overshadowed everything. The surgeon knew it and just could not face it.

Her first words, 'I know I'm dying!' sounded challenging, petulant and disappointed, because she felt cheated by all the 'good dying guides'. She had done the best she could to help herself and felt let down when she felt no better. Her mistake, however, was to see her life as over when there was still life to be lived. She had cancer, and would die – as we all will – but she was still vital and lively. One of the roles of the psychoanalytic psychotherapist is to talk and listen to the life in an individual while acknowledging that deathly impulses can overwhelm and obliterate all hope. The therapist's role in talking and listening to the patient is to change the subject – from death to life. Although this woman used the future tense, the vehemence of her exclamation indicated that she was still very much in the present and that there was potential for thinking about the disease in the present too, not in terms of it having beaten her already!

It would be wrong to generalise about cancer and its effects on the individual. We are all different and some cancer patients do not have the time or the opportunity to think about how the disease is affecting them, consciously and unconsciously, or how they might prepare for their death. However, with many others, for whom there is treatment and even cure, there is the possibility of change. This is the essence of this book. Having cancer is not necessarily a decline into passivity and then agonising death. It is not true that cancer is a physical invader of the body – a parasite – but it is true that cancer acquires a special, grotesque meaning in the mind that requires close consideration and understanding. As this book has tried to show, it is possible for a person suffering from cancer to have a more vital, even optimistic, perspective on their illness, and it is imperative that doctors and nurses learn to appreciate the emotional devastation that cancer wreaks on the sufferer. Doctors and nurses must learn to listen more and prescribe less. Of the other professional group I have considered – psychoanalytic psychotherapists – much more could be said, but what I have argued is for the analyst to move beyond the preciousness and religiosity of traditional private practice and move into the sphere where psychoanalysis can have great benefit. Psychoanalytic principles applied creatively by therapists working on the cancer wards would have a dramatic effect on the morale of the patients and of the doctors and nurses treating them.

A creative life can be lived with cancer and its treatment. Being diagnosed with cancer is not the end and concentrating on the disease as a death sentence rather than an opportunity to understand its effects on the psyche is a sure way to bring the end closer and more swiftly. The cancer patient, like all of us, should go to a good death and, as Epicurus said, a good death is a good life. The art of a good life and a good death are the same; it is about achieving integration and fulfilment.

Bibliography

Antonelli, F., ed. (1977) *Therapy in Psychosomatic Medicine*, Rome: L. Pozzi, The Proceedings of the 3rd Congress of the International College of Psychosomatic Medicine, Rome, 16–20 September, 1973: 'Psychotherapy with Cancer Patients', pp. 717–740.

Bion, W.R. (1961) *Experiences in Groups and Other Papers*, London: Tavistock Press.

—— (1967) 'Notes on Memory and Desire', *The Psychoanalytic Forum*, 2: 272–273, 279–280. Reprinted in E. Bott Spillius ed., *Melanie Klein Today*, London: Routledge, 1988.

—— (1970) *Attention and Interpretation*, London: Tavistock Press.

—— (1992) *Cogitations*, London: Karnac Books.

Bohr, N. (1934) *Atomic Theory and the Description of Nature*, Cambridge: Cambridge University Press.

Bohr, N. (1958) *Atomic Physics and Human Knowledge*, London: Chapman & Hall.

Cannon, W.B. (1957) 'Voodoo Death', *Psychosomatic Medicine*, 19(3): 182–190.

Day-Lewis, T., ed. (1995) *Last Letters Home*, London: Macmillan.

Department of Health/Welsh Office (1995) *A Policy Framework for Commissioning Cancer Services* (the Calman–Hine Report), London: NHS Executive.

Ellershaw, J., & Ward, C. (2003) 'Care of the Dying Patient: The Last Hours or Days of Life', *British Medical Journal*, 326: 30–34.

Elliot Smith, G. (1916), 'Shock and the Soldier', *The Lancet*, 2: 813–817.

Elliot Smith, G. & Pear, T. (1917) *Shell Shock and Its Lessons*, Manchester: Manchester University Press.

Entralgo, P.L. (1955) *Mind and Body. Psychosomatic Pathology: A Short History of the Evolution of Medical Thought*, trans. A.M. Espinosa Jr, London: Harvill.

Fallowfield, L. (1995) 'Psychosocial interventions in cancer', *British Medical Journal*, 311: 1316–1317.

Freud, S. (1915) 'Thoughts for the Times on War and Death', *Standard Edition of the Complete Psychological Works of Sigmund Freud*, Vol. 14, pp. 289–300, London: Hogarth Press.

—— (1916) 'On Transience', *Standard Edition of the Complete Psychological Works of Sigmund Freud*, Vol. 14, pp. 303–307, London: Hogarth Press.

—— (1926) 'Inhibitions, Symptoms and Anxiety', *Standard Edition of the Complete Psychological Works of Sigmund Freud*, Vol. 20, pp. 87–156, London: Hogarth Press.

Gabor, D. (1960) *Inventing the Future*, London: Encounter.

Goldie, L. (1956) 'Hypnosis in the Casualty Department', *British Medical Journal*, 2: 1340–1342.

—— (1961) 'Attention and Inattention in Neurophysiology', *Nature*, 192: 1116–1121.

—— (1974) 'The Role of the Psychiatrist in Obstetric Therapeutics'. In D.F. Hawkins, ed., *Obstetric Therapeutics*, London: Bailliere Tindall.

—— (1978) 'Psychiatric Aspects of Otolaryngology', *The Practitioner*, 221: 701.

—— (1981) 'Psychosomatic Aspects of Gynaecology; Psychosexual Problems; The Menopause'. In D.F. Hawkins, ed., *Gynaecological Therapeutics*, London: Bailliere Tindall.

—— (1982) 'The Ethics of Telling the Patient', *Journal of Medical Ethics*, 8: 128–133.

—— (1983) 'Doctors in Training and the Dying Patient', *Journal of the Royal Society of Medicine*, 76: 995.

—— (1984) 'Psychoanalysis in the National Health Service General Hospital', *Psychoanalytic Psychotherapy*, 1(2): 23–34.

—— (1985) 'The Interdisciplinary Treatment of Cancer: Co-operation or Competition?' *Psychosocial Oncology: Proceedings of the British Psychosocial Oncology Group*, 1986.

—— (1989) 'Psychological Aspects of Pain Perception and the Memory of Pain' and 'Too Much Pain: The Emotional Problems Associated with Serious Illness and Its Treatment'. In B. Keplinger & H. Smid, eds., *Pain-Research and Treatment*, pp. 1–5 and pp. 128–132, respectively, Linz: Selva Verlag.

Harvey, P. (1997) 'Minding Body and Soul', *Health Service Journal*, 13 (November): 28–29.

Hernandez-Peon, R., & M. Donoso (1960) 'Influences of Attention and Suggestion upon Subcortical Evoked Electrical Activity in the Human Brain', *Proceedings of the First Congress of Neurological Science*, London: Pergamon Press.

Janssen, P. (1999) *Psychoanalytic Therapy in the Hospital Setting*, London: Routledge.

Joseph, F. (1962) 'Transference and Countertransference in the Case of a Dying Patient', *Psychoanalytic Review*, 49: 21–34.

Keizer, B. (1997) *Dancing with Mister D: Notes on Life and Death*, London: Doubleday.

Kissen, D.M., & Le Shan, L.L. (1964) *Psychosomatic Aspects of Neoplastic Disease*, London: Pitman.

Klein, M. (1963) *Our Adult World and Other Essays*, London: Heinemann.

Kubler-Ross, E. (1969) *On Death and Dying*, New York: Macmillan.

Le Shan, L. (1969) 'Mobilising the Life Force', *Annals of the New York Academy of Science*, 164: 847–861.

—— (1977) *You Can Fight for Your Life*, New York: Evans & Co.

—— (1989) *Cancer as a Turning-Point*, New York: Dutton.

Le Shan, L.L., & Gassmann, M.I. (1958) 'Some Observations on Psychotherapy with Patients Suffering from Neoplastic Disease', *American Journal of Psychotherapy*, 12: 723.

May, C. (1998) 'Lord Moran's Memoir: Shell Shock and the Pathology of Fear', *Journal of the Royal Society of Medicine*, 91: 95–100.

Menzies, I.E.P. (1961) *The Functions of Social Systems of the Nursing Service of a General Hospital*, Tavistock Pamphlet, No. 3, London: Tavistock Clinic.

Mount, B. M., Jones, A., & Patterson, A. (1974) 'Death and Dying: Attitudes in a Teaching Hospital', *Urology*, 4 (6): 741–748.

Shelford, C.F.G. (2003) 'Risk, Statistics and the Individual', *British Medical Journal*, 237: 757.

Spiegel, D. (1994) *Living Beyond Limits*, New York: Ballantine/Fawcett.

—— (1995) 'Essentials of Psychotherapeutic Intervention for Cancer Patients', *Support Care Cancer*, 3: 252–256.

Spiegel, D., & Bloom, J. (1983) 'Group Therapy and Hypnosis Reduce Metastatic Breast Carcinoma Pain', *Psychosomatic Medicine*, 45: 333–339.

Spiegel, D., Bloom, J., Kraemer, H., & Gottheil, E. (1989) 'Effective Psychosocial Treatment on Survival of Patients with Metastatic Breast Cancer', *The Lancet*, 2: 888–891.

Spiegel, D., Bloom, J., & Yalom, I. (1981) 'Group Support for Patients with Metastatic Breast Cancer', *Archives of General Psychiatry*, 38: 527–533.

Spiegel, D., & Lazar, S.G. (1997) 'The Need for Psychotherapy in the Medically Ill', *Psychoanalytic Inquiry*, 17: 45–50.

Steiner, G. (1975) *After Babel. Aspects of Language and Translation*, London: Oxford University Press.

Trijsburg, R.W. et al. (1992) 'Effects of Psychological Treatment on Cancer Patients: A Critical Review', *Psychosomatic Medicine*, 54: 489–517.

Young, M., & Cullen, L. (1996) *'A Good Death': Conversations with East Londoners*, London: Routledge.

Index